The Ultimate Guide to Psychedelics

Evil Temptresses or Miracle Cures For Treating Depression, Anxiety, and PTSD?

Myra Grayce

© **Copyright 2021 - All rights reserved.**

The content contained within this book may not be reproduced, duplicated, or transmitted without direct written permission from the author or the publisher.

ISBN: 978-1-7776904-1-0

Under no circumstances will any blame or legal responsibility be held against the publisher, or author, for any damages, reparation, or monetary loss due to the information contained within this book, either directly or indirectly.

Legal Notice:

This book is copyright protected. It is only for personal use. You cannot amend, distribute, sell, use, quote, or paraphrase any part, or the content within this book, without the consent of the author or publisher.

Disclaimer Notice:

Please note the information contained within this document is for educational and entertainment purposes only. All effort has been executed to present accurate, up-to-date, reliable, complete information. No warranties of any kind are declared or implied. Readers acknowledge that the author is not engaged in the rendering of legal, financial, medical, or professional advice. The content within this book has been derived from various sources. Please consult a licensed professional before attempting any techniques outlined in this book.

By reading this document, the reader agrees that under no circumstances is the author responsible for any losses, direct or indirect, that are incurred as a result of the use of the information contained within this document, including, but not limited to, errors, omissions, or inaccuracies.

Table of Contents

Introduction 1
   The Psychedelic Renaissance 3

Chapter 1: The Secrets of MDMA 9
   What is MDMA? 9
   History and Traditional Use 11
   Studies and Interesting Findings 13
      The Boston Group 14
      The Secret Chief Leo Zeff 15
      ARUPA 16
      Ann Shulgin 18
      Sallie Kueny 19
      Claudio Naranjo 20
      George Greer's Contribution 21
   Big Pharma and the Banning of MDMA 23
      Merck's Attempt to Clear Their Name 24
   MDMA Today 26
      MDMA & Depression 27

    MDMA & PTSD 28

    The Effects of Self-Dosage MDMA 31

    MDMA Precautions 33

  Dosage Guide 35

Chapter 2: The Magic in Magic Mushrooms 37

  What are Magic Mushrooms? 37

  History and Traditional Use 39

  Studies and Interesting Findings 40

    Timothy Leary: From Harvard to Hedonist 40

    Leary's Concord Prison Study 45

    Johns Hopkins University Research Trials 49

    The Research of Psilocybin for Therapeutic Purposes 51

  Big Pharma and the Banning of Magic Mushrooms 54

    The Legal Status of Psilocybin in Different Countries 56

  Magic Mushrooms Today 58

    The Risks of Experimenting With Psilocybin Without Supervision 58

    Thomas Chan: I am God 60

    COMPASS Pathways and the Study of Psilocybin 62

    Microdosing With Psilocybin 63

  Dosage Guide 69

  What is LSD? 71

  History and Traditional Use 73

    Ergot on Rye and the Salem Witch Trials 73

The Discovery of LSD 75

LSD, the CIA, and Mind Control 77

Studies and Interesting Findings 81

The Contribution of Dr. Sidney Cohen 81

Studies on LSD and Behavioral Patterns 83

LSD Studies Focused on Autism and Social Anxiety 85

A Groundbreaking Neurological Study on LSD and Brain Activity 86

LSD and MDMA: A New Super Combination? 89

Big Pharma and the Banning of LSD 91

The Counterculture Catalyst 92

LSD Today 94

Becoming an Underground LSD Guide 96

Dosage Guide 97

Chapter 4: The Truth About DMT 99

What is DMT? 99

History and Traditional Use 103

Studies and Interesting Findings 105

Stephen Szára Taking the First Step 105

Rick Strassman and the Spirit Molecule 105

DMT for Major Depression 108

DMT for Substance Abuse Disorders 110

Yes, the Spirit Molecule is Also Being Tested as a Remedy for Stroke 112

Big Pharma and the Banning of DMT 114

DMT Today 117
   We Need to Talk About DMT and Serotonin Syndrome Disorder *119*
Dosage Guide 121

Chapter 5: All-Natural Ayahuasca 123

What is Ayahuasca? 123
   Ayahuasca Goes by Many Names *124*
History and Traditional Use 125
   The Westernization of Ayahuasca *129*
Studies and Interesting Findings 132
   The Church of Santo Daime *132*
   Clinical Studies: Ayahuasca and Drug Addiction *132*
   Ayahuasca Can Help You Grow New Brain Cells *135*
   The Benefits of Ayahuasca Backed by Research *137*
Big Pharma and the Banning of Ayahuasca 139
   The Story of **Gonzales v. O Centro Espírita Beneficente União do Vegetal** **140**
Ayahuasca Today 142
   Need-To-Know Information About Ayahuasca Use *144*
Dosage Guide 147

Chapter 6: What's Inside Peyote? 149

What is Peyote? 150
   Deconstructing Peyote *150*
   Peyote and its Many Names *152*

History, and Traditional Use 152
   The First Experimental Ventures 154
   Peyote: From Recreational Use to Secret State Shenanigans 156
Studies and Interesting Findings 158
   The Preservation and Sustainability of Peyote 158
   The Appeal of Peyote 159
   Peyote as an Antibiotic 160
Big Pharma and the Banning of Peyote 160
   The American Indian Religious Freedom Act 161
   The Native American Church and Their Rights in Canada . 164
Peyote Today 167
   What Peyote Does to Your Mind and Body 168
   Create The Best Setting for Your Own Peyote Ritual 169

Glossary of Terms 173
   Addiction Research Center Inventory 173
   Breakthrough Therapy Designation 174
   Constraint-Induced Movement Therapy 176
   Hallucinogen Rating Scale 179
   Drug Enforcement Administration Mission Statement 179
   Investigational New Drug Process 181
   MAOI 185
   Pharmacodynamics 186
   Pharmacokinetics 187
   Pharmacology 188

United States Scheduling Procedures and Guidelines 189

Visual Analog Scale 191

Conclusion 195

The Psychedelic Renaissance in Full Swing 195

MDMA 196

Magic Mushrooms 196

LSD 197

DMT 197

Ayahuasca 198

Peyote 199

References 201

Images 213

Introduction

How much do we really know about psychedelic drugs or substances? One well-known fact is that some of them occur organically in nature, and some of them are developed and produced in laboratories. And because we are so clever, with some, you can even do both. The word *psychedelic* is classified as a neologism or a newly invented word that consists of other, more established, and older words. It is derived from a combination of Greek words, which is a combination of the words *dēloun* (to reveal or make visible) and *psychē* (soul), which gives one a much deeper insight into the neologic quotient of these words. From this perspective, we can see how accurately it describes the effect psychedelics have on the human experience after it is consumed. The term 'hallucinogenic' is also commonly used; however, it does not carry the same depth if you look at the origin and construction of the word 'psychedelic' from this perspective.

The use of psychedelic substances has influenced some of the most famous literary words and art in history and sparked countless research endeavors to find each type's purpose. Humphrey Osmond coined the term itself after he was in touch with Aldous Huxley. The latter famously wrote an entire literary work called *The Doors of Perception* while under the influence of mescaline. Before the true purpose of psychedelics can start to be recognized by scientists, medical professionals, and the public—which is still a work in progress—the research on these substances first had to overcome a twenty-plus year rift marked by the counterculture movement and the popularity of the recreational use of psychedelic substances. These behaviors caused psychedelics to fall out of favor with law enforcement and the government, and their use was outlawed.

The revival of psychedelic research and its credibility can be credited to three countries, namely Switzerland, Germany, and the United States. However, although Pharmaceutical companies like Merck and Sandoz were initially involved in developing and producing some of these substances, Big Pharma has kept its distance from this newfound revival. Their unwillingness to participate is a debatable topic but one worthy of exploration.

There is evidence that plant-based psychedelics have been used throughout history for different ailments and ritualistic purposes. This culture of self-medicating still exists today alongside the culture of recreational use of psychedelics (Carhart-Harris & Goodwin, 2017).

The big question is, what should we believe about psychedelics? Are they going to make you see the devil, or can they help improve the quality of life for many individuals across the world? The mainstream opinion about psychedelic drugs is still very much tainted, and for a good reason. They say too much of anything is a bad thing. If you are going to look at the current cultural representatives of psychedelics like Timothy Leary and Terence McKenna, among others, you'll see that they advertise these substances as part of a hedonistic and alternative spiritual lifestyle, almost like that's the only place it can ever belong.

INTRODUCTION

Not everyone wants to make a cosmic connection, and if this is the only reference they have about psychedelic substances, then their reluctance to embrace it is understandable. However, as independent pharmaceutical institutions and companies are looking into these curious substances' therapeutic effects, they see the same potential that researchers saw decades ago. Now, with more advanced medical equipment and technology, there really is a way for us to find out if psychedelic drugs have any therapeutic potential. The revolution has already begun.

The Psychedelic Renaissance

The Psychedelic Renaissance has been coming for some time as independent laboratories and researchers have been testing psychedelic substances to look for answers to some of humankind's most significant mental issues. Still, this reality first hit the public in February 2014 when the publication *Scientific American* featured an editorial that strongly opposed the banning of psychedelic substances and called for the unbanning of research on psychedelic substances. Whoever wrote this editorial knew that there was, and is, mind-blowing preliminary evidence from research that points to the fact that psychedelic drugs can cause a revolution in the pharmaceutical industry.

One must admit that the public reputation of psychedelics during the past half a century or more has been a rollercoaster ride, to say the least. First, these substances were a novel discovery that showed therapeutic potential. However, they were subsequently demonized as harmful substances that turn people into lunatics and damage their brains. Only now do researchers reassess the previously suggested potential of psychedelic substances for their positive effects on our health. So many things happened that put psychedelics in a bad light—many public figures advertised these substances as a recreational means to achieve a "cosmic connection." Psychedelics and its supporters have had to fight for the movement to experience a chance at a clean slate and a renewed reputation.

In the past, the American culture did not have this firm opposition towards psychedelics. In the '50s and '60s, they were merely introduced as a new class of drugs that required further research to establish its therapeutic and medicinal pros and cons. Every possible angle was researched, including lab studies, psychotherapy, and medical assessments. Most of the findings of these studies were promising, even though some were still in their embryonic stages. Some of the most forthcoming researchers in psychedelics were Harvard University's Timothy Leary and Richard Alpert. However, their gaze shifted towards the recreational use and alternative approach to psychedelics, which caused an upheaval in government and the public and the subsequent banning of all substances. All that was left of the research was the newly created stigma.

This hostile attitude towards psychedelics has been the status quo for the past few decades. That is, until MAPS, or the Multidisciplinary Association for Psychedelic Studies, was founded by Ricks Doblin to mark the start of the Psychedelic Renaissance. Established in 1986, MAPS is a nonprofit advocacy group dedicated to the education and research of psychedelics and focused on conquering the legal and scientific obstacles that prevent further scientific research in psychedelic substances. MAPS is now known as the organization that kick-started the renaissance movement, at least according to most experts on the matter. So, if you didn't know before, you know now. We are in the middle of the Psychedelic Renaissance, and there is mind-blowing research happening at independent pharmaceutical facilities across the world to help individuals deal with debilitating conditions like depression, addiction, PTSD, autism spectrum disorder, and even existential anxiety related to terminal illness.

Many of these research endeavors are in their primary stages, but what has been found by conducting basic testing and observation is promising. This carefully constructed guide to psychedelics and all their dimensions will take you on a journey covering six stigmatized psychedelic substances to discuss their structure, history, and how and why millions have misunderstood them for so many years.

Another valid question concerning psychedelics, their nature, and their use is why have these substances been misunderstood for so long? Many say that the banning of psychedelic substances is not due to their danger to individuals or society but because they pose a threat to the Big Pharma industry, which monopolized the drug industry and may lose a lot if their investors are drawn to the "greener pastures" of new treatments with more effective and longer-lasting effects. If you think about it, why would harmful and harsh treatments like chemotherapy, which has a significant mortality rate and horrible side effects, quickly and efficiently move through the prescribed clinical trial phases when substances like psilocybin and LSD, which have almost no connection to any fatalities, are being held back with an air of skepticism? What scientists and researchers are facing today is overcoming the stigma of psychedelic substances that was created during the last 60 or more years in the cultural war America waged against these substances. This war, fuelled by the media, is what mostly caused this stigma that we are still aware of when it comes to these substances, even though some of them, like DMT, have been proven to be endogenous to the human body.

Thinking back on the scientists who started believing in psychedelics, one can deduct that they began to conduct tests and experiments not because they had all the information we have now, but because they believed these substances have significant therapeutic potential (Bell, 2017). Matt Lamkin aptly wrote in *Scientific American* that psychedelic medicines and treatments are starting to look like a viable component of future medical care and treatment but that the law has definitely not reached an equal point that can help make these treatments available yet. He reasons that "The prospect of psychedelic drugs gaining approval as treatments will force a reckoning for our existing system of drug control" (Richtert, 2019). And if there's one thing the law does not want to do, probably for a good reason, is to admit that they were wrong and their regulatory approach may have caused more harm than good. In the end, it was the recreational use of psychedelics, its links to cult activity and other spiritual endeavors, and also the abuse of these substances that helped create the stigma around psychedelic drugs.

It is speculated that the Psychedelic Renaissance is owed to institutions like MAPS we mentioned above as well as the Heffner Research Institute, but also other factors that are not as easy to spot as an outsider in the world of medical and drug research. Other factors that helped this movement happen are a change in personnel at the FDA who were replaced with a 'newer generation of drug regulators. This is according to the Heffter Research Institute's cofounder David Nichols, who is also a professor emeritus in pharmacology at Purdue University. So, out with the old stiff ones and in with the newly-educated and flexible ones. That would always be a great help. Another journalist, Andrew Brown, also wrote in the *Spectator* that psychedelics as a concept have become more serious and there is now a visible line between medical and pharmacological research on psychedelic substances and, as Andrew

Brown calls it, the "wackier end of the pro-LSD lobby" (Richtert, 2019). Here, we find ourselves within the Psychedelic Renaissance, and to understand it, one must understand the past, the present, the substances themselves, and the politics that have been upon them.

Chapter 1:
The Secrets of MDMA

Even though MDMA was created for the sake of helping improve other medicine, it twisted into a sinister operation that later became a trendy party drug. It's an interesting journey, but one that asks whether this substance has healing properties or why legislation has passed to classify it as illegal. The therapeutic benefits of MDMA may surprise you after reading this chapter, and you may even wonder why MDMA can't be used in the way it was intended.

What is MDMA?

MDMA, also known as Ecstasy, Molly, or X, is pharmaceutically known as 3,4-*methylenedioxymethamphetamine*. According to some sources, MDMA was developed to be an appetite suppressant, and although it was patented by Merck & Co., a pharmaceutical company, the substance was not actually approved for release. It is a synthetically created substance used to distort sensory perceptions and evoke feelings of wellbeing. MDMA is usually available in a capsule or tablet that can be multicolored and can even have cartoon-like figures printed on them. When MDMA is referred to as 'Molly,' people are usually talking about a crystalline-like powder that is encapsulated rather than being in tablet form. Some individuals believe that using Molly is safer than using MDMA in tablet form. This belief, however, is not valid, and having this conception about Molly can be dangerous. Molly, specifically, is often mixed with other substances like bath salts or methamphetamine, turning it into a whole new cocktail with unknown side effects. The side effects of normal MDMA include an increased heart rate, nausea, chills, blurred vision, a feeling of faintness, and tension in the muscles.

When MDMA or 'Ecstasy' is ingested, the substance increases serotonin and norepinephrine production and then blocks the brain's ability to reabsorb it. These are essential neurotransmitters, or chemical messengers, in the brain that are associated with feelings of general wellbeing and happiness. Serotonin plays a central role in behavior as it assists in regulating sleep, mood, appetite, an individual's sense of pain, and other defining characteristics that can lead to personality or behavioral changes. It is because of the sheer excess of serotonin being released in the brain, combined with no reuptake reaction, that causes elevated moods, an overall sense of wellbeing, and a loving and peaceful sensation. This superfluous release of serotonin becomes problematic when the brain's serotonin supplies become scarcer and scarcer, and it leaves the individual with a feeling of deep depression when the effects of the MDMA have worn out. At the same time, the secretion of the neurotransmitter dopamine also increases in the brain, and the stimulation of the central nervous system gives the user a feeling of elevated energy levels, a heightened sense of self-awareness, a sensation of happiness, and a reduction in a person's social inhibitions in general. Although Ecstacy does not cause hallucinogenic effects like LSD, paranoia is a known side-effect of the drug.

MDMA has quite a variety of street names apart from X or Molly, including *Stacy, Malcolm X, E, rolls, Adam, Mandy* (specifically popular in the UK), *the love drug, happy pill, Mollie*, and *beans*.

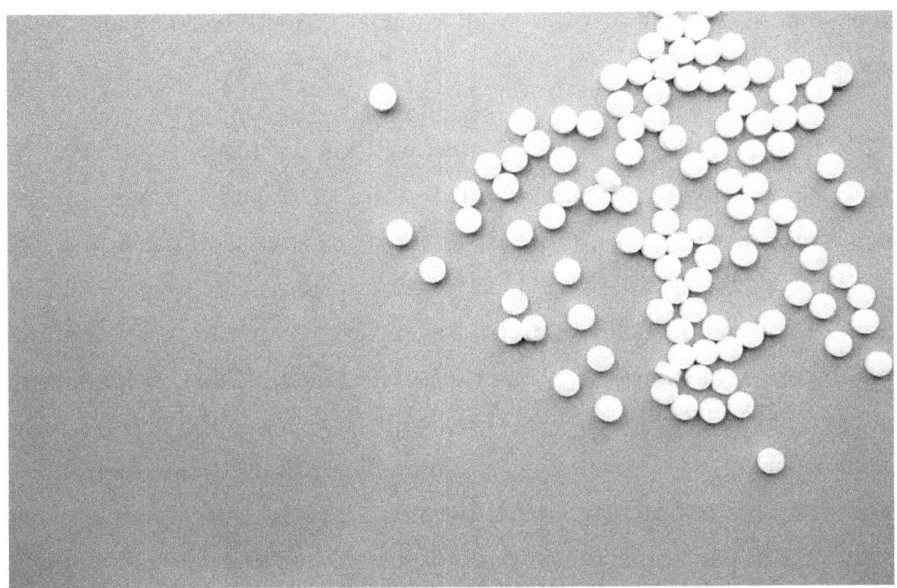

History and Traditional Use

After MDMA's initial development in 1912, the substance again became popular among some psychiatrists during the late 1970s and even the early 1980s. The psychiatrists who supported the use of MDMA included famous author and chemist, Alexander T. Shulgin. Shulgin believed that using it during therapy enhanced the patient's ability to communicate effectively and to develop an insight into their own psychological problems. These initial experiments and research endeavors occurred before MDMA was evaluated by the FDA, the U.S. Food and Drug Administration, and during this time, the substance also became more freely available to the public on the street—one method through which was as a psychotherapy treatment.

This is where MDMA's traditional use took a turn and became used for something that is more well-known to most individuals—as a recreational drug.

MDMA, or Ecstacy, is probably most well-known for its use at raves or rave concerts, which became popular in the 1970s and 1980s in Europe and the United States—more or less at the same time the popularity of Ecstasy began to rise. These parties would take place in old or abandoned buildings, like warehouses or factories, or in a more natural environment like a forest. Other users who made MDMA famous were supporters of the New Age Movement, who used the substance to explore their own emotional and mental states between themselves and others, attempting to reach the mystical states of awareness that are described in some ancient religions. For the New Age movement's followers, Ecstasy was to be the precursor to a new revolution of neuro consciousness. A sense of harmony and peace characterizes the rave and electronic music culture, and many followers of the rave culture movement feel that there is also a spiritual level to this. Ecstasy is taken at these concerts to create a feeling of euphoria and enhance the user's own sensory perception as they listen to the music, see the bright colors, and look at the colorful light displays. Ecstasy's ability to cause overheating in the human body has been the cause of several deaths at these types of events—even at some high-profile events like the annual Electric Daisy Carnival.

Studies and Interesting Findings

The FDA made its first decision to approve MDMA-related research trials in the 1990s. One notable trial the FDA approved involved human experimentation with the aim being to determine Ecstasy's effect on pain relief in terminally ill patients. Research was also conducted to see if Ecstasy can serve as an additional treatment for psychotherapy, as was thought decades earlier. The outcomes of these studies have yet to be published decades later; however, what these earlier studies did achieve was to establish MDMA's safety specifications and restrictions for the administration of the substance in a clinical trial setting. There are also studies where MDMA is used to determine its therapeutic effect on Post Traumatic Stress Disorder, or PTSD, in autistic adults who suffer from anxiety, and for patients who suffer from terminal illnesses such as cancer.

Research on rodents also revealed that high dosing has other negative effects on serotonin and the brain. After about a week or two of giving large doses of MDMA to rodents, roughly three to four doses a day, a decreased expression of the serotonin transporter was already visible. This transporter is a protein-related to the recycling of released serotonin. On top of this, the rats also indicated changes in the gene expression that is responsible for tryptophan hydroxylase regulation, and this enzyme plays a vital role in the synthesis of serotonin.

In a nutshell, these low levels of serotonin are linked with depressive moods and poor memory and are consistent with studies on humans that showed regular MDMA use causes confusion, anxiety, paranoia, depression, and an inability to concentrate properly. Apart from that, it has also been shown that MDMA has degenerative effects on norepinephrine as can be seen in cognitive impairment, excitability, and euphoria (Winstock, 2016).

These are some of the main reasons why MDMA was banned by the FDA, even though it is still widely used as a recreational drug. However, studies have continued on this mysterious substance, and new scientific research appears to have identified a quality that was last associated with MDMA in the early 1900s—its healing potential.

The Boston Group

There was a group of individuals known as the "Boston Group" who showed an immense interest in the therapeutic potential and effects of MDMA, and their vested interest had a longstanding influence on MDMA's therapeutic application, starting in 1976. It was a diverse group that consisted of several followers of psychotherapy and spiritual development, a chemist, and some individuals who were linked with the MIT Artificial Intelligence Lab. Their view of MDMA was therapeutic and based on this perspective, they systematically synthesized MDMA and distributed the drug throughout the Boston area. There were even some early MDMA therapists, like the physician Rick Ingrasci, who got his supplies from the Boston Group. Some researchers of the history of this group are firmly convinced that the Boston Group distributed MDMA on bona fide grounds with the idea that they cared about the individuals who were using the drug and the experience they had with it.

The Secret Chief Leo Zeff

Leo Zeff is another prominent name in the world of therapeutic MDMA, and as a psychotherapist, he invested his interest in the use of psychedelics. Zeff practiced psychotherapy in the '60s, and he started experimenting with LSD as a form of treatment. When Alexander Shulgin started with his 'trials' during the '60s, Zeff got wind of this practice through Shulgin's associate named Tony Sargent. LSD famously became illegal in 1966, but this did not stop Zeff as he just continued his work with psychedelics in therapy underground. This caused an informal underground network to develop where Zeff was known to share useful information with other members of this network, and for this role, he earned the name "the Secret Chief." However, he was only introduced to MDMA in 1977, when he started to conduct his own therapeutic work with the substance. The Secret Chief was responsible for administering MDMA to over 4000 individuals over the next 12 years and training more than 150 'therapists' in his methods.

Zeff continued to conduct therapy sessions based on spiritual and personal development, and these sessions had a notable consistency in their structure. The sessions would always start on a weekend, specifically a Friday night, where patient-participants would congregate in a "talking circle" and spend time together. They would take turns in telling the rest of the group where they were in their life's journey. After each participant said their part, Zeff outlined the rules of the therapy session. These rules included prohibiting aggressive behavior or doing anything to harm yourself or anyone else, leaving the therapy site without consent, and having any type of sexual contact or sexual relations with another patient/participant. The participants would then be required to pledge that, if Zeff ordered them to stop doing something they are busy with, they needed to comply immediately. Zeff used tools like headphones and eyeshades to keep participants focused on their inner selves and not on each other. The drug sessions were done during the day, and the group would eat together afterward in the evening. The final part of each session happened on Sunday, where a ritual of sorts was conducted. Participants were to integrate their experiences by sharing them along with any insights they may have gained from the extended therapy session.

ARUPA

ARUPA is an acronym for *The Association for the Responsible Use of Psychedelic Agents* and was founded at the Esalen Institute at Big Sur in California. The term was coined by one of the founders of the Esalen Institute, Richard Price, and this famous institute was a center that focused on the development of new techniques in psychotherapy during the '70s and '80s. The interesting thing about the acronym ARUPA is that it comes from Sanskrit and is dubbed as a "formless" network.

Thus, ARUPA had no structure it adhered to, and it mainly focused on organized meetings on an invitation-only basis with the aim to discuss the therapeutic abilities of psychedelic substances. The reason ARUPA is mentioned is that MDMA became a hot topic of discussion during these meetings in the '80s. Participants in these meetings included some of the most prominent supporters of these alternative therapeutic methods, including Leo Zeff, of which we previously spoke, George Greer, and Alexander Shulgin. In 1985, the Esalen Institute held the largest known conference about MDMA and its role in psychotherapy. There were 35 attendees who were all considered experts in the field of psychedelics as a form of therapeutic treatment, and after the conference, the group concurred on several points.

They believed that administering MDMA to patients had the potential to reduce the patient's natural defensiveness and fear of emotional harm and thereby opens the patient up to express their feelings in a more direct and honest way. These individuals are also more accepting of both criticism and praise. They can recall lost memories, specifically of past trauma, which subsequently brings them closure and relief. Discussions to integrate MDMA as part of psychiatric treatment were part of the discussion during this conference. (Passie, 2018).

This is an early example of scientists and medical professionals studying MDMA and its therapeutic effects, keeping the ethics of their practice in mind. However, there are more examples of individuals who showed an interest in MDMA's therapeutic potential.

Ann Shulgin

Ann Shulgin, the wife of the notorious chemist Alexander Shulgin, became involved with MDMA as a lay therapist after she started using it in therapy sessions with patients. There were even cases where she administered MDMA to herself along with the patient during sessions, but she realized that this method didn't work and abandoned it. Under the instruction of Leo Zeff, Shulgin partnered up with a licensed therapist, who recommended her to patients who had undergone more than six months of therapy. These patients had the option of undergoing an MDMA session with Shulgin, and she adopted some of Zeff's methods, including his 'rules' a patient had to agree to before starting a session. Shulgin administered an oral dosage of 125mg of MDMA to her patients, and for some, a second optional dosage of 40mg was administered 90 minutes later into the session.

One concern Shulgin had with MDMA as a therapeutic treatment is she observed that patients sometimes came into contact with a sense of darkness, or their own "dark side," which they were not prepared for, or even more so, were terrified of. She insisted that patients discuss all their issues with her openly before starting a session because of the sheer darkness she noted in some of their experiences. However, Shulgin was convinced that if the darkness is embraced by its owner, it can become an ally and bring relief to the subconscious mind. Despite her concerns, she also believed that this could only be achieved through therapy using MDMA.

Shulgin did not have a lengthy career in this field, but her work was influential, and she contributed by authoring an early guide to the use and methods of MDMA therapy. Although she was a supporter of using MDMA along with therapy, Shulgin admitted that its use is not applicable in all cases.

Sallie Kueny

Chemist Alexander Shulgin had many fingers in the pie that was MDMA studies and research. One of these fingers was involved in the initiation of an exploratory study in 1979 at the Pacific Graduate School of Psychology in San Francisco, California. It is here where psychologist Sallie Kueny conducted an important test by administering MDMA to 9 patients in what can be described as a 'nonclinical' setting—this would typically be the patient's home environment. The aim was to evaluate the use of MDMA in the field of psychotherapy, while specifically focusing on what is called the "therapeutic alliance" between the therapist and the patient. The therapeutic alliance refers to the relationship between the patient and the therapist, its nature, and its importance as a tool for the success of the therapy.

The report on the study was never published, but it included a formal research protocol, a synopsis of the sessions, and a follow-up after nine months. Each participant was to receive three administrations of MDMA. However, after the first session with the administration of the drug, the plug was pulled on the study due to technical reasons. Kueny still had a conclusion to make based on the brief period that this study was active. First, no negative effects were detected during or after any of the nine sessions. Additionally, all of the participants had positive feedback, including that they had the ability to free themselves from anxiety. Kueny concluded that the evidence gathered from the brief study substantiated the requirement for further studies on the matter regarding the massive therapeutic potential in the use of MDMA.

Claudio Naranjo

Claudio Naranjo is considered an early researcher of MDMA and its therapeutic properties. As a Chilean psychiatrist and medical doctor, Naranjo often visited the United States through scholarships, calling himself an "eternal student" during the '60s. After completing his studies, he started working at the *Centro de Estudios de Antropologia Medica* in Santiago, Chile as a research psychiatrist. Soon enough, Naranjo became an associate of the famous Alexander Shulgin, and this association led to them working together, testing MDMA in '65 and '66 at the research center where Narajo was working in Santiago. Naranjo subsequently published a book covering the topic of drug-assisted psychotherapy.

As time went by, Naranjo became a well-known figure in the world of psychotherapy. In the latter part of the '70s, he was considered a key figure in teaching programs about psychotherapy and spirituality and was one of the most highly educated practitioners in this field. This is significant as these were the early phases of development for drug-assisted psychotherapy. Naranjo also met Zeff during the '70s and was one of the participants of the ARUPA meetings held at the Esalen Institute along with Leo Zeff and others that were considered experts during that time. Naranjo experimented with both MDA and MDMA, and by 1984, he had used MDMA as a therapeutic element on over 30 patients. MDA, considered to be a close relative to MDMA, was considered by Naranjo to be a more dangerous option in therapy, and he deemed MDMA to be less toxic, showing significantly milder side-effects when used in psychotherapy. He also did not consider MDMA to be hallucinogenic. He was reported as saying that he uses MDMA as a tool for "opening up" as it helps him to gain a wealth of information he would otherwise have not been able to get from the patient if fully conscious. Naranjo was determined to individualize his approach in the field of psychotherapy.

According to Naranjo, the basic approach when implementing MDMA in therapy was based on the same method as when using LSD; however, he worked a little differently, wanting to take the use of this substance further by healing relationships. His focus, therefore, was to conduct therapy sessions on groups of individuals who had ongoing relationships with one another. His purpose was to get rid of unhealthy feelings, or as he calls it, 'unhealthy garbage,' that may have built up between individuals in order to heal and strengthen the relationship (Passie, 2018).

In Naranjo's opinion, using MDMA in this approach worked well because MDMA creates that feeling of emotional openness, empathy towards those around you, and interpersonal trust. These effects bring people closer together and create a positive emotional experience between them. He found this form of group therapy successful and noted that it did not cause any form of chaos or misunderstandings, but rather a basic structure that keeps all participants involved in the group and protects their experiences from any form of invasion (Passie, 2018).

George Greer's Contribution

George Greer's interest in MDMA started when he was a student in the '70s. His exposure to MDMA as a tool in psychotherapy began when he attended one of the ARUPA conferences in 1975 at the Esalen Institute. In 1979, Greer opened a private practice in San Francisco, and the next year he became aware of the Secret Chief Leo Zeff, with whom he had a few training sessions on how to use MDMA with therapy.

Greer came to the conclusion that if MDMA was used or prescribed by a physician, it was not illegal because it was considered therapeutic use under the supervision of a medical professional. According to him, he studied the regulations regarding MDMA use and concluded that if he manufactured it himself, he could legally prescribe and administer it to patients during therapy. All he required was informed consent and a peer review. This conclusion and subsequent action led to Greer treating over 80 patients with MDMA after manufacturing his own MDMA in Alexander Shulgin's laboratory. With the assistance of his wife and registered psychiatric nurse, Requa Tolbert, he conducted his MDMA-facilitated psychotherapy. Unlike Naranjo, Greer used the more traditional LSD-based method and treated the subjects at their homes, incorporating eyeshades and background music the patients listened to using headphones. If the session was interpersonal of nature, the headphones would be excluded, and the music would be played in the background.

Greer and his wife, Tolbert, took the same advice from Leo Zeff that Ann Shulgin did when she developed her method, and they laid down some ground rules for the patient. For example, all patients have to stay on the premises where the session is taking place until there is an agreement that the session has ended. Other, now familiar rules included no sexual contact, no destructive behavior towards yourself, others, or the property, and that patients must follow the instructions given by the therapist. Greer and Tolbert also included a brief prayer, which, in their opinion, assisted their patients to change their mental state to one of surrender. The wording they used was from a poem originally composed by the French Catholic Priest named Francois Fenelon.

Greer's most notable contribution to the study of MDMA as a therapeutic aid in psychotherapy happened in the form of an informed decision. He made this decision once he caught wind in 1982 that MDMA was being used recreationally in parties, realizing that this would inevitably lead to the drug being scheduled, so he decided to document his work. In 1983, he self-published his research and shared it with a small selected group of psychotherapists. This paper gives invaluable information about the treatment methods, dosages used, and side effects, if any, that were present during the therapy sessions he led. The conclusion of the research, which involved 29 patients, stated that 23 of these patients reported notable, positive changes in their demeanor between 1 week after therapy and the two-year follow-up.

In 1993, Greer became the co-founder and Medical Director of the Heffter Research Institute, which was founded for the purpose of further studies on psychedelics (Passie, 2018).

Big Pharma and the Banning of MDMA

Amid an extensive DEA Scheduling Hearing between 1984 and 1988, the DEA placed an emergency ban on MDMA in 1985 after it became available to the public on the streets and became increasingly popular as a recreational drug. Ecstasy was subsequently placed on the Schedule 1 list of drugs. Ever since this decision was made in 1985, MDMA has remained on that list except for a brief period between 1987 and 1988. The DEA Scheduling Hearing's decision was for MDMA to remain a Schedule 1 Substance.

Merck's Attempt to Clear Their Name

Merck, the pharmaceutical company that, according to most sources, is the creator of MDMA, appears to be unsure about how they became negatively associated with this drug, even though most sources have the same account of this history and the reason for its creation. For example, another version of the story is that the drug was created to suppress the appetite of soldiers in the German Army. According to this account, the substance was revoked after human test subjects started showing very unfavorable and strange side effects. After a squadron of soldiers started to make faces and remove their shirts when the marching band played, scientists decided that this drug may not be suitable for further testing. The German press got hold of this story and had a field day with it, and ultimately, the story was reported in medical reports and cited in textbooks. In these test cases, apparently embryonic MDMA was used.

The development of MDMA for the purposes of being an appetite suppressant and testing on German soldiers are just a few of the stories behind MDMA's blurred history. To clear their name of these rumors which have been plaguing the company for so long, Merck wanted to do another investigation almost a century later. According to extensive research they've conducted at their headquarters in Darmstadt, Germany, Merck is claiming the widespread story of their experiment with MDMA on German soldiers to be a myth.

After researchers scoured patient documents, medical reports, and other data, they found that MDMA was developed to help stop bleeding by encouraging a blood clotting process. The reason Merck was developing this type of medicine was to beat their main competitor, the pharmaceutical company, Bayer, who had the leading product for this specific treatment during the time Merck was developing MDMA. Of course, the pharmacologists at Merck wanted their version to be more effective, and as a result, they developed MDMA. They did this by using chemicals in their formula that differ from Bayer's product, which also allowed them to avoid a disagreement that could result in a legal battle over Bayer's drug's patent.

To further substantiate their findings, Merck also claims their investigation proves that they did not test the substance on any German soldiers. Merck adds that, when MDMA was developed around 1912, it was not tested on human or animal subjects. Animal testing only started more than a decade later. The latter research and experimental testing were led by chemist Max Oberlin who was employed at Merck after he discovered the original MDMA patent in 1927. Oberlin's tests were, however, short-lived as the chemicals he used in his experiments became too expensive. Oberlin made an interesting comment about the nature of MDMA, which was that, to him, it was similar to adrenaline.

Thus, according to Merck, MDMA was administered to humans for the very first time in the 1950s when the US Air Force conducted secret tests using MDMA, among other drugs. Merck claims that, according to their own research, the first human testing conducted by them occurred in 1959.

Subsequently, MDMA became a well-known drug and landed in the hands of the chemical company, Dow, who synthesized the drug, and a former scientist started the first *recorded* human trials of MDMA by testing the drug on himself (Deutsche Welle, 2006).

MDMA Today

Currently, researchers are looking into the effects of MDMA on conditions like PTSD, depression, mood disorders, and chronic pain with an air of confidence that separates their approach from the previously underground efforts. What also sets past research apart from new research is that it was conducted by individuals that were not as specialized and knowledgeable as the scientists and pharmacologists who are looking into MDMA's effects today. However, after decades have passed since this substance was banned, new hypotheses have started to emerge and subsequent research is being initiated—surprisingly without the involvement of any Big Pharma companies. It appears that Big Pharma has decided to avoid and even ignore these research expeditions to some extent.

Previously, multiple studies were discussed along with what researchers learned about the therapeutic use of MDMA using specific methods within their ideological paradigms. Many of the studies produced the same results, and these results were insightful, even against the background of all the negative physiological side-effects that have also been recorded during animal and human studies. In the end, modern medical science paints a promising picture of MDMA use for medicinal practice just like the vision seen by researchers in the '70s and '80s, Current research will no doubt be more adaptive and scientifically evolved to identify any issues that may not have been pinpointed by the MDMA pioneers of the '70s and 80s. Next, we'll present recent research outcomes using MDMA as a medical or therapeutic treatment and a projection for the near future.

MDMA & Depression

Research on MDMA and depression has indicated that one of the biggest pros MDMA has for treating depression is how quickly it starts to relieve symptoms. This relief is because of MDMA's ability to cause an increase in norepinephrine, serotonin, and dopamine in the brain, which leads to an improved mood and state of mind. In comparison to most traditional antidepressants which are classified as selective serotonin reuptake inhibitors (SSRIs) and take at least 6 weeks before showing any clear improvement in mood. In a 2012 study focused on the therapeutic effects of MDMA on depressive symptoms, researchers selected 40 participants and placed half in a control group and half in the MDMA group. Even if a participant only had a predisposition to developing depression, the MDMA dosing clearly indicated significant improvement in these participant's mood and symptoms, compared to those in the control group. Researchers did note that, for MDMA to become an acknowledged way of treating depression, further studies need to be conducted to establish whether it can be used as a long-term solution for those who suffer from it.

Another study looked at teenagers who have been using MDMA for an extended period of time and who are battling suicidal issues. This study was conducted based on the known fact that, after taking MDMA, serotonin levels can be left reduced in the brain, which can lead to suicidal thoughts or actions. This study from 2011 surveyed over 90,000 adolescents and teens between the ages of 12 and 17 and the study concluded a notable link between MDMA use and suicide attempts. In the end, suicide rates were shown to be nine times higher among teens who have taken MDMA than those who have never taken any illicit drugs. It's probably not unreasonable to assume that suicidal tendencies can also be related to an absence of knowledge about safe MDMA dosages in these cases. In a controlled study, MDMA is administered as part of the study, and the dosage is controlled by those conducting the research. Further study on safe dosage levels may indicate that suicidal tendencies are not an inevitable outcome of MDMA use for therapeutic purposes. What these two studies show regarding the use of MDMA is that the dosage administered or taken and its frequency may have a significant impact on whether MDMA can be used as a therapeutic drug.

Another critical study regarding the safe use of MDMA was conducted to investigate serotonin toxicity. For example, administering MDMA to a patient with a mental illness who is already taking other psychiatric drugs may cause dangerous side effects. Studies have found that mixing MDMA with antidepressants can cause a level of serotonin toxicity in the brain due to both of these substances' effects on serotonin production. It is very important to note that taking MDMA with another antidepressant can cause adverse side effects such as a very high body temperature, feelings of confusion, and agitation, and it can even lead to coma and subsequent death (Sissons, 2020).

MDMA & PTSD

One of the most recent trials studying the effect of MDMA on Post Traumatic Stress Disorder was conducted by the Multidisciplinary Association for Psychedelic Studies (MAPS) in San Francisco using pure, lab-produced MDMA that has not been cut using another substance. The dosages used on participants were also altered according to their specific needs. MAPS hopes to develop MDMA, very much like it was used in the past, not as a drug that can fix the issue on its own, but as a component that can be used in conjunction with psychotherapy in order to help individuals who have PTSD.

Eric Sienknecht, a psychologist for MAPS, believes that MDMA has the ability to 'unlock' the trauma PTSD patients' own minds cling to and free them from the devastating effects of this disorder. Sienknecht's hypothesis is startlingly similar to those of the psychotherapists and researchers who worked with and used MDMA decades ago. He believes that an individual who is under the influence of MDMA can access memories that are so traumatic, they are hidden in the deepest, darkest corners of the mind. The fantastic part of this is that, while under the influence of MDMA, a patient will re-experience a traumatic event that has been tormenting them and causing debilitating symptoms, and during this revisiting, they will have clarity of mind and even the ability to think creatively in order to deal with and understand the memory. This is what leads to healing—allowing your mind to show you the trauma instead of trying to hide it from you, which leads to such complications as PTSD. With the help of MDMA, the patient has the clarity of mind to deal with the most traumatic experiences which are disabling them in everyday life.

Despite Sienknecht's theory, there are still many medically trained professionals who disagree. Some, however, concede that MDMA can possibly be used as a last resort if no other psychiatric drugs or treatment is successful (Abo, 2020).

It's almost like it's happening all over again. Medical professionals have been conducting small-scale studies on the effects of MDMA in small groups spread across the United States. These researchers believe that the use of MDMA in therapy can help not only individuals with PTSD but also those who have suffered sexual assault, violent crime, and those who have mental illness. Currently, new approval from federal regulators allows the drug to be used in more extensive clinical trials, which means that MDMA can soon become medicinally legal.

Phase III trials, funded by MAPS, are the final trials required by the FDA before MDMA can be considered an approved and legal prescription drug. The Phase III trial follows the "Phase I" and "Phase II" trials, which were both randomized, double-blind, placebo-controlled, and multi-site trials. On July 28, 2016, the FDA and MAPS reached an agreement regarding the Special Protocol Assignment relevant to the Phase III clinical trials. This agreement between MAPS and the FDA focuses on planned conducts, clinical endpoints, the protocol design, and a method of statistical analyses of the trials, and indicates that there is an agreement that all of these points are acceptable regarding the support of the FDA's regulatory approval (MAPS, 2017).

The Phase III trials involving MDMA-assisted psychotherapy that is conducted by MAPS started in September 2018. Sixteen sites are used, and candidates are from Canada, the United States, and Israel. This trial is expected to be successful, and researchers are expecting FDA approval by 2021; however, as is common in studies, extensions are necessary due to unforeseen circumstances that may arise in the process of the study. According to researchers and medical professionals who have worked on MDMA-assisted psychotherapy studies, several pharmaceutical medications have been used in conjunction with prolonged periods of psychotherapy; however, none have yielded results where patients were ultimately cleared of their previous symptoms and no longer met the diagnostic criteria for PTSD (Gustin, 2020).

Chapter 1: The Secrets of MDMA

If the results of these studies are so dramatic and so promising, why would Big Pharma not seize the opportunity to partake in the research process? MDMA has proven to be one of the most versatile treatments for several mental conditions when administered correctly and in suitable circumstances. This is not a myth anymore—it is solidly backed by decades of research and studies. It appears that sometimes lab creations that are meant to treat one ailment can become a miracle cure for another.

The Effects of Self-Dosage MDMA

Research has found that an individual who ingests MDMA without supervision or knowledge of the drug will most likely have the following experiences that can also have specific acute effects:

1. After ingestion, the individual will start experiencing the effects of Ecstasy in about 45 minutes. This is when a single dose is taken. The individual will experience extroversion, a sense of warmth and empathy towards others, a need or a strong willingness to talk about emotional experiences they can vividly recall, and a heightened sense of wellbeing. Another key effect of MDMA is that users experience an enhanced sense of sensory perception, which makes everything seem "ultra-real" and makes them feel like they are in the moment during every moment. These are probably the reasons why the use of MDMA at rave and dance parties has become so popular. However, the adverse effects are also significant and can be very dangerous.

2. An MDMA overdose that leads to death is not a common occurrence, but the human body can suffer severe damage from

taking too much MDMA or taking it too often in high dosages. If an overdose of MDMA is not fatal, it can cause other complications like high blood pressure, panic attacks, faintness in the body, and even seizures and loss of consciousness.

3. An important aspect regarding MDMA to keep in mind is that it is a type of stimulant, so it has the ability to dehydrate, as well as cause the individual who ingested the substance to start taking part in a vigorous activity like dancing. If vigorous activity occurs for extended periods of time in a warm environment, it can cause hyperthermia, where the body's core starts to heat up and the body loses control of its ability to conduct normal temperature regulation to keep its organs healthy. Hyperthermia requires immediate treatment as it immediately starts breaking down muscle tissue and causes an electrolyte imbalance which will wreak havoc to the kidneys. On top of all this, vigorous exercise will cause individuals who ingested MDMA to start drinking lots of liquids. Because MDMA causes your body to retain water, the extra liquid intake can cause brain swelling and electrolyte imbalance. In other words, increased physical activity while having the substance in your system is a huge cause for concern.

4. For several hours after ingestion, the individual will have trouble making judgments regarding skilled or complex activities, like driving a car, and should avoid doing so.

5. Other side effects include clenching of the jaw, which is an involuntary action, a sense of self-detachment or depersonalization, and a lack of appetite. Less common sub-acute effects include depression and aggressive behavior.

The above side-effects come from self-dosing, meaning the individual most likely took a medium to high dosage of the drug. For recreational purposes, a medium dose is a 100-150mg ecstasy pill, and a high dose is considered to be 300mg or higher (Winstock, 2016). Studies and trials associated with dosage including tests on primates and rodents indicated that, if a moderate to high dose was administered twice a day for a period of four days, the nerve cells that contain serotonin are damaged. The effects could still be seen in the primates that were tested even seven years later. Reduced numbers of serotonergic neurons were observed, which indicated long-term and permanent damage.

MDMA Precautions

Due to the fact that MDMA has some interesting side effects, it's always good to know under which circumstances one shouldn't take it. All hallucinogenic substances contain alkaloids, which are mainly found in plants; however, they are most commonly responsible for the trippy effect you get from these substances. Also, considering that a substance like MDMA will be going down your intestinal tract and coming in contact with your liver, there are other substances that you should not mix with MDMA in order to prevent damage to your organs.

1. Alcohol

    Because MDMA in itself causes your body temperature to rise and your body to become dehydrated, mixing it with alcohol, which also dehydrates your body, can cause severe dehydration. What can make this even worse is that, due to the fact that MDMA has a stimulating effect on the body and the brain, it can cause you to want to drink more. If your drink of choice is going to be alcoholic beverages, you can put your body in a dangerous situation. Research also suggests that ingesting both MDMA and alcohol can place your heart under unnecessary stress. Alcohol in itself has an adverse effect on your body, so ingesting it with a substance that has chemical components you are unfamiliar with may have negative effects on your health.

2. MAOIs

    MAOI stands for monoamine oxidase inhibitor and can inhibit the breakdown of neurotransmitters like serotonin, dopamine, and noradrenaline, which increases the concentration of the neurotransmitter in the brain. MAOIs are also well-known antidepressants, so if you are aware of the fact that you are taking an antidepressant that is classified as an MAOI, you need to avoid MDMA. Mixing the two substances can cause a near-fatal reaction in your brain where your serotonin levels become way too high.

3. Drugs that are all metabolized through the same enzyme in the liver called CYP2D6 have the potential of interacting in an unfavorable manner. Examples of these drugs include any opiate derivatives, DXM, which is found in ecstasy tablets that are not considered pure, codeine, and Prozac. By consuming any combination of these drugs that are metabolized by the enzyme CYP2D6, the metabolization process is going to take longer, and the effect is that the individual who consumed the substances is going to feel like they took a much higher dose of the drugs.

4. You can put yourself in a life-threatening situation if you take MDMA with any antiviral or antiretroviral drugs, which are known as protease inhibitors. These drugs act as inhibitors that stop a virus from replicating.

It is important to ensure the purity of the MDMA you are taking and to not take MDMA more than once every three months. For individuals suffering from depression, the recreational use of MDMA is not recommended even though it has very promising outcomes in a therapeutic environment (Reality Sandwich, 2019b).

By now, you might see that MDMA is a misunderstood substance that should be approached properly when used recreationally, and it carries a huge potential for therapeutic treatment purposes. Should MDMA be a Schedule 1 drug? We'll leave that up to you to decide.

Dosage Guide

The recreational guidelines are all amounts that you'll find in high-quality ecstasy tablets. It's important to ensure that you don't buy MDMA that's been laced with other substances if you want to get the best results. For microdosing, a crystalline or powder is preferred so the substance can be measured with higher accuracy.

Recreational Dose	80 mg (standard)	150 mg (high)
Microdose	200 µg (small)	5–25 mg (standard to high)

Chapter 2:
The Magic in Magic Mushrooms

If you've heard of the counterculture movement, the hippies, or Timothy Leary, then you have most likely heard of psilocybin, more commonly known as *magic mushrooms*. This natural hallucinogenic has a highly stigmatized background; however, researchers are trying to break this mold in order to show the world its versatility and healing potential. If research is to be believed, this substance is truly one of nature's miracles and, if used with caution and care, can improve the lives of millions of individuals who suffer from a variety of mental or neurological conditions. The story of psilocybin is an interesting one and, as with any other psychedelic substance, it can also be used and abused for other means. Familiarize yourself with what psilocybin really is and what it may be capable of.

What are Magic Mushrooms?

Magic mushrooms can grow in the wild, or they can be cultivated, and they contain the substance *psilocybin*, ($C_{12}H_{17}N_2O_4P$), which is an all-natural hallucinogenic and psychoactive ingredient naturally present in these fungi. From a chemical perspective, psilocybin is classified as an indole hallucinogen, also known as *Benzopyrrole,* referring to a heterocyclic and organic substance that can also be found in flower oils like orange blossom and jasmine, surprisingly in coal tar, and, strangely enough, in fecal matter. Often, when talking about the chemical components of magic mushrooms, psilocybin and psilocin are mentioned. The main difference between the two is that psilocybin contains phosphates that are attached to the oxygen atom's molecule. These mushrooms can be found in South America, Mexico, and also in the northwestern and southern regions of the United States. Psilocybin is classified as a tryptamine or an indolealkylamine, and its structure is very much like that of *lysergic acid diethylamide* (LSD). It is known to be abused by individuals to initiate a mental "trip" in order to have a hallucinogenic and euphoric experience. This experience is possible because the chemical compounds in the substance have direct interaction and effect on the central nervous system (5-HT) or serotonin receptors.

One of the fascinating things about magic mushrooms is that there are more than 180 types of these mushrooms that have been happily growing in nature for most of our known history, most notably the Mexican species *Psilocybe mexicana* and *P. cubensis* (formerly known as *Stropharia cubensis*). No wonder they have been used in rituals and ceremonies; although there is an ongoing debate about the how's and when's as some believe their earliest use was in northern Africa. Today, psilocybin is also produced synthetically in laboratories. When used recreationally, a popular way to take magic mushrooms is to lace them with LSD for an extra bamboozling effect (Drugs.com, 2021).

Magic mushrooms can be prepared before consumption by drying them, but they are also consumed fresh and used for cooking, making tea, and can even be mixed with cannabis or tobacco for smoking. There is also a liquid form that usually comes in a small vial and is a

Chapter 2: The Magic in Magic Mushrooms

light, clear brown color. This psychedelic drug is one of the few that is 100% natural and not necessarily created in a laboratory. They can be physically described as similar to other mushrooms you'd buy at a grocery store—whitish-grayish in color with long stems, dark-brown caps, and a light color in the center.

If you want to get some magic mushrooms, you have to know the lingo. This fungus has a complete portfolio of nicknames that include *mushies, golden tops, philosophers' stones, liberties, amani, shrooms, blue meanies,* and *agaric*.

When you consume magic mushrooms, the hallucinogenic element in the fungi can make you hear things and experience sensations that are not real. However, because the effects of magic mushrooms are believed to be influenced by environmental factors, consumption may not always lead to the same type of experience. Consuming magic mushrooms also has some potential side effects, which include drowsiness or extreme relaxation, nausea, excessive yawning, paranoia and panic, anxiety, psychosis, and some introspective experiences (Hartney, 2012; Drugs.com, 2021).

History and Traditional Use

Although magic mushrooms are believed to date back as far as 9000 B.C., Western Society discovered their effects in the mid 20th century. It all started when a mycologist named R. Gordon Wasson was making his way through Mexico with the aim to study and gather information about mushrooms. Little did he know that he was going to discover an incredibly unique mushroom on his trip. He came into contact with the Mazatec, which is an indigenous people who live in the Southern parts of Mexico, in the Oaxaca region. Upon meeting these people, he participated in a ritualistic ceremony that was conducted by a Mazatec Shaman and which involved the consumption of magic mushrooms. After he returned home, he wrote an article about his experience, and it was promptly published in one of Life Magazine's 1957 editions. At this point, Wasson had not identified psilocybin yet. Psilocin and psilocybin were identified and extracted from one of the mushrooms brought back from Mexico with the help of one of Wasson's colleagues, Roger Heim, and the man known as the "father of LSD," Albert Hoffman.

Timothy Leary is a name synonymical with magic mushrooms and other psychedelic substances. He happened to read the Life magazine article that Wasson wrote and it fascinated him. He decided to start experimenting with magic mushrooms at Harvard University. It is at this point where magic mushrooms were irrevocably associated with the hippie movement of counterculture and their search for new spiritual experiences (Freeman & Chandler, 2009).

Studies and Interesting Findings
Timothy Leary: From Harvard to Hedonist

Timothy Leary's transition, from being a Harvard University psychologist, to a countercultural icon and considered "the most dangerous man in America," was quite drastic. It depicts what could happen when an individual, especially one of influence or renown, decides to use psychedelics for recreational and social use. Nevertheless, Leary is considered a legend and will always be closely associated with the use of magic mushrooms. His story is a fascinating one.

Leary, who was a renowned psychologist at Harvard University, received his doctorate in psychology in 1950 from the University of California at Berkeley. He stayed there as an assistant professor until 1955 when he left the university. In the field of psychology, Leary famously developed an Egalitarian model for the patient-psychotherapist relationship, one founded on the principles of mutual respect. He also developed and promoted novel techniques of conducting group therapy, and published a system for the classification of interpersonal behavior. With his sterling reputation in the world of academics, he was appointed as a lecturer in 1959 at the Ivy League institution Harvard University.

It was at Harvard where Leary started to develop an interest in the psychedelic substance psilocybin after reading about its discovery. He hypothesized that psychedelic substances can have the powerful potential to influence, and even expand, an individual's state of consciousness, and that they also have personality transformation potential. He found himself a like-minded ally in fellow psychologist, Richard Alpert, and together they started the *Harvard Psilocybin Project*. The two psychologists started administering psilocybin to graduate students at the academic institution and went on to share the substance with a few well-known artists of that time, which included writers and musicians. Instead of looking at the medically-related potential of psilocybin, Leary wanted to explore its cultural and philosophical significance. In these early stages of research on the newly-discovered psilocybin, most researchers wanted to keep its use within a small and elite group; however, Leary had other ideas. He believed that the experience of taking this psychedelic substance should be introduced to the public, and his focus was specifically on younger people (The Editors of Encyclopedia Britannica, 2020).

Because Leary's approach and methods in his experiments were seen as controversial and unacceptable by the small group of researchers and the university, Harvard dismissed both him and Alpert in 1963. Part of the reason they were dismissed was because of a student named Andrew Weil, who tried (and succeeded) to discredit them by saying that they administered psilocybin to undergraduate students despite an agreement to refrain from doing so. The dismissal from Harvard seemed to free Leary from academic shackles and opened up opportunities for him to conduct experiments the way he wanted to.

While residing in his Millbrook mansion in New York during the '60s, he formed and became the center of a small community that lived a hedonistic lifestyle. It was during this time that Leary also started experimenting with LSD, and he started traveling and giving speeches and lectures on campuses, supporting the use of psychedelic drugs. He became famous and acquired a highly public profile with his slogan of "turn on, tune in, drop out." This became the slogan of the counterculture movement. United States President Richard Nixon called Leary the "most dangerous man in America," and many researchers of psychedelic substances felt that Leary was delegitimizing their studies, making them seem ridiculous and less credible.

Leary, who passed in 1996, left some interesting literature that shows the nature of his interest in psychedelic substances. One of the most relevant is called *The Psychedelic Experience: A Manual Based on the Tibetan Book of the Dead*, which he co-authored in 1964 with Ralph Metzner and Richard Alpert, and it discusses rituals belonging to the *Bardo Thödol*, or Tibetan Funerary Texts, and their employment while using hallucinogenic substances. These rituals, or meditations, were originally meant to guide the spirits of those who have recently passed and were used with psychedelic substances to help the user through a phase called ego obliteration and into a state of transcendence (The Editors of Encyclopedia Britannica, 2020).

To fully understand Leary's philosophy about the use of psychedelic substances in rituals, and his intentions regarding *The Psychedelic Experience*, one needs to understand what ego obliteration entails. Ego obliteration can also be understood as ego death, and the purpose of this is to stop yourself from being controlled by your own ego, your identity, and your sense of self. The reason why many counterculture followers believed in ego obliteration is that they believed that, if you let your ego guide you, you will only be able to see things in opposites; left and right, black and white, war and peace, and love and hate. They believed that humans are capable of a broader experience that is not bound to these limitations. Thus, if you allow your ego of self-identity to guide you through life, you will always look at life through the lens of duality and never be enlightened. It is also believed that being guided by your ego can only make you miserable as a human being because looking at the world through a lens of right and wrong can cause resentment and anger.

There is a general consensus that to reach ego death, one must go through seven stages. This will release you from the cuffs of your ego and open you up to new spiritual experiences. Leary appeared to believe that psychedelic substances like LSD and psilocybin are a mandatory component of reaching ego death.

1. Stage one of ego obliteration is the spiritual awakening. This first step has an existential nature as you need to start by asking yourself about your purpose in life, the reason you are living,

and what you are really supposed to do while you are alive. These questions may come more naturally if you are experiencing bouts of depression or if you have experienced a loss of some kind. When you start to feel a nagging void in your life is when the spiritual awakening begins.

2. After the spiritual awakening comes what is called the Dark Night. During this time, the individual is supposed to reach the deepest part of their depression, which comes from the existentialist doubt and frustration that caused their Spiritual Awakening. During the Dark Night, the individual becomes isolated because they don't understand the meaning of their own life.

3. The Dark Night then leads to a journey of Exploration where the individual starts to expand their spirituality into the esoteric, or more unknown, branches of experience after being unsatisfied with normal branches of religious practices.

4. If the individual commits themself to the exploration of these esoteric branches of spirituality, they will get their first Glimpse of Enlightenment, which is also known as *satori*. This glimpse may be experienced as terrifying; however, the individual should not allow it to be a deterrent and should move forward to reach the next step.

5. The fifth step, if the terror of that glimpse can be conquered, is the growth of the soul. Growth refers to the maturing of the soul and the first feelings of letting go of that which always seemed to hold you back—your ego.

6. The next step is to surrender yourself and your spirit. Let go of everything that is connected to your ego and trust the unknown in order to become who you are meant to be.

7. The final step in order to reach ego death is to ensure that you have a new sense of awareness after growth, surrender, and development in awareness, have taken place spiritually. This is what makes the individual evolve beyond the limits of their ego.

For Leary, the use of psychedelic substances like psilocybin was crucial for this seven-step process, which he incorporated into the Tibetan *Bardo Thödol*. According to those who practice this kind of meditation, there are many ways or pathways that lead to ego obliteration, including the Bhakti, Jnana, and Raja forms of yoga. There is, however, a consensus between these individuals that psilocybin is the fastest way to achieve this form of enlightenment—almost like a shortcut.

Leary had no intention of developing psilocybin for medicinal or therapeutic purposes that could help existing medical conditions. His story is, however, relevant in order to explain the powerful mind-altering effects psychedelic substances like psilocybin can have when used for other purposes in an uncontrolled environment.

Leary's Concord Prison Study

While still at Harvard, Timothy Leary conducted one of the most famous psilocybin experiments related to a possible reduction in recidivism rates. This experiment was conducted before Leary went off on his hedonistic and spiritual psychedelic ventures, and the study has a very interesting hypothesis. There has also been a follow-up study conducted more than thirty years later to look at the long-term effects of Leary's study and if there were any successes in the methodology applied. The experiment itself lasted for about two years.

The original Concord Prison Experiment was inspired by the preliminary research on psilocybin conducted at Harvard for its subjective therapeutic treatment potential. In this study, it was recorded by Leary and his associates that 88% of the subjects reported learning something valuable about the world and about themselves, and 62% reported that the psilocybin treatment made a positive change in their lives (Doblin, 1998). Some subjects even experienced spiritual or mystical effects that can be compared, according to the researchers, to a religious conversion. Due to the outcome of this preliminary experiment, Leary hypothesized that psilocybin can be used as a platform for behavioral change, specifically in individuals with a history of criminal offenses.

Coincidentally, similar experiments were also conducted using LSD on incarcerated sex offenders in California and in the Netherlands; however, these experiments were not conducted with the aim to reduce recidivism but only to change behavioral patterns, thought patterns, and personality changes.

Conducted by a team at Harvard University and directed by Timothy Leary, the original Concord Prison Experiment ran between 1961 and 1963. The aim of the study was to use and evaluate psilocybin-assisted group therapy to assess the reduction rates of recidivism in the Concord Prison. The researchers aimed to completely avoid the normative "doctor-patient," "researcher-subject" approach, but rather followed a group program based on collaboration. The study involved 32 inmates, who were all incarcerated in the Massachusetts Correctional Institute, or Concord, which is outside of Boston and not too far from Harvard University. All subjects were willing participants, and most of them were closely approaching their parole dates, which made them ideal for the study.

The reason Leary chose recidivism is to test the effects of psychedelics on actual behavior and to test how effective it is in changing behavior, as he thought this type of study would carry more weight than mere questionnaires or other similar tests. Conducting research on inmates' behavior was a more practical method, and as these individuals were let out on parole, which is a legal process in itself, there were no legal issues regarding the safety of the study when it came to conducting experiments on these people and then releasing them from a controlled environment. Before the group therapy began, each inmate completed three standardized tests that evaluate psychological functioning. These tests, which are the Thematic Apperception Test (TAT), the California Personality Inventory (CPI), and the Minnesota Multiphasic Personality Inventory (MMPI), were also to be conducted after the group sessions to measure progress. The group therapy consisted of four participants in each group and two research associates. The entire span of the experiment was about six weeks and consisted of bi-weekly meetings. At the meetings, psilocybin was administered twice to every inmate. During the group sessions, they openly shared their experiences with consuming psilocybin. Some of the subjects viewed the administration of psilocybin as a challenging experience, so in an effort to show solidarity, the research executive or group leader would also take the substance with them in an attempt to build trust and a sense of healing. Once subjects' parole dates were close, they would start engaging in discussion on how they would approach life outside prison.

Post-release group meetings were not originally included in the planning of the experiment; however, they were identified as a necessary component to help released individuals integrate back into society and stay out of prison. Freedom Inc., a nonprofit organization, was created to help keep in touch and support the participants of the experiment, but Leary himself admitted that nowhere near enough planning went into the post-release phase. A type of halfway house needed to be established where former inmates could meet to discuss their experiences and struggles very much like an Alcohol Anonymous association would function.

When the follow-up study was conducted, it was clear that there were promising elements, especially with the administration of psilocybin to alter the behavior of inmates; however, it was also clear that the study did not go as planned due to a lack of post-release support. In the original reports, there was an emphasis placed on post-release support and group programs, but the follow-up study found that one of the reasons this experiment did not follow through to reach the desired results was because these post-release groups and programs were not available to the participants who were released. Once more, Leary admitted to this fault in the experiment. Looking back, there were definitely positive points linked to the use of psilocybin in the Concord Prison Study, even though the follow-up study identifies the same drawback as Leary did himself, which is a lack of post-release support.

Researchers still believe that this unanswered question about the effectiveness of psilocybin on changing behavior is worth investigating and that a new experiment can be justified (Doblin, 1998). Leary's idea to conduct a more practical human experiment with psilocybin in order to showcase its potential was a brilliant idea, and identifying inmates who are eligible for parole posed a challenging task, as they would by no means have been easy to reform. In other words, the initial idea and hypothesis of the study aimed at bringing the potential of psilocybin as a therapeutic tool to the forefront were scientifically brilliant. Researchers today re-identify that brilliance and they aim to rectify the parts where Leary's experiment went wrong in a true trial-and-error fashion.

Johns Hopkins University Research Trials

Roland R. Griffiths, Ph.D., a psychopharmacologist and professor at the Department of Psychiatry and Behavioral Sciences and the Department of Neurosciences at the Johns Hopkins University School of Medicine, started the psilocybin research program just shy of 20 years ago. He started conducting research by testing the effects of psilocybin on volunteers who had a generally healthy profile. Griffiths' research studies at Johns Hopkins University were the first to receive regulatory approval in the United States, which gave them the green light for re-initiating research on psilocybin in 2000. Griffith published a study in 2006, widely considered a landmark study, that caused a renewed interest in the research of psychedelics on a global scale. He didn't stop there, of course. Since his landmark publication, he has published more groundbreaking research studies in over 60 peer-reviewed articles, all in scientific journals. Since its inception 20 years ago, the Johns Hopkins research program has studied psilocybin and conducted research by administering it to more than 350 healthy voluntary patient-participants, and about 700 sessions have been held.

Now, Griffiths is the head of an all-new *Center for Psychedelic and Consciousness Research* at Johns Hopkins Medicine. This center is unique in that not only is it the first of its kind in the United States, but it is also the largest of its kind around the globe. The center became a reality due to a $17 million donation from donors who remain private, but who are also invested in developing and advancing this field of research on psychedelics for therapeutic use and for the improvement of health. Its purpose is to look at the potential of psychedelics like psilocybin with the aim to find alternative ways for individuals to cope with their mental health and to ultimately look for properties and methods that can lead to healing. Griffiths argues that, because of the demonization of psychedelic drugs like magic mushrooms in the '60s and '70s, especially by the media, these research processes and breakthroughs had to be postponed due to restrictive regulations placed on them by the US government.

The next step for the center is to start researching the effects of psilocybin on individuals indicating early symptoms of Alzheimer's disease. Researchers, including Griffiths, believe that, as the drug has been proven to have an effect on neuroplasticity—the brain's ability to reorganize and form new synaptic connections which can lead to cognitive changes—it may have an effect on cognitive processes that involve the development of Alzheimer's disease.

Acute treatment using psychedelics instead of using chronic treatment of psychotropic (pharmaceutical) drugs and ongoing therapy have been likened to a corrective surgical procedure. The example Griffiths uses here is a joint replacement; a procedure that only needs to be done once and that has lasting, changing effects. To medical professionals, especially psychiatrists who have been treating chronic mental illness or disorders in patients with psychotropic drugs, this may seem completely irrational or impossible. However, a magnitude of tests have been conducted, and these substances appear to have that potential (Jefferson, 2019).

A trial focusing on the same topic was conducted in the form of a randomized, double-blind trial at John Hopkins University in 2016, and researchers found that administering a single dose has the potential to improve the patient's life quality. The results also indicated a significant decrease in anxiety and depression in patients that had an advanced stage of cancer which could include a terminal diagnosis. The words "substantial improvement" were used to describe the outcome of this particular research study.

Another research study conducted at Johns Hopkins University involved the treatment of 51 adults who were all diagnosed with advanced cancer. They were initially administered a small dosage of psilocybin and, five weeks later, they received a higher dose. The study included a six-month follow-up. The results indicated that about 80% of the patients that participated in the study reported significant feelings of relief from anxiety and depression, and these feelings of relief lasted for up to the entire six-month period.

Studies regarding psilocybin at Johns Hopkins University now have a broader focus and include testing the substance's therapeutic effects on conditions like opioid addiction, Alzheimer's disease, PTSD, anorexia nervosa, alcohol abuse in individuals who suffer from major depression, and even post-treatment Lyme Disease syndrome, which was previously known as chronic Lyme disease (Drugs.com, 2021).

The Research of Psilocybin for Therapeutic Purposes

An interesting fact about psilocybin is that it is just about a hundred times less potent than LSD. However, this does not mean it is not a powerful tool that can be used for therapeutic and medicinal purposes. In order to understand how psilocybin can be used as a medicinal or therapeutic tool, and for which conditions, one must look at the history and current progress of its research.

First, from a broad perspective, this substance has shown signs of successfully treating a wide range of mental conditions that include obsessive-compulsive disorder (OCD), depression, nicotine addiction, alcohol addiction, cluster headaches, and cocaine addiction, and it also appears to aid in the psychological distress a patient experiences when diagnosed with cancer or other terminal illnesses. In recent months, orchestrated initiatives have been noticed in locations such as Colorado and Oregon with the aim to make psilocybin legal. These initiatives may not be enough, however, but research is pushing forward to prove that the substance is worthy of FDA approval.

Research about the medicinal and therapeutic use of psilocybin is conducted mainly by the Heffter Research institute which, as we know it now, focuses on the study of psychedelics and is founded by George Greer. Greer explains the purpose of researching these substances very eloquently by highlighting that the purpose is not only to understand them but also to get to know the human brain and how it functions in order to subsequently reduce suffering and pain with psychedelic substances. The Heffter Research Institute is currently focusing on two specific research hypotheses surrounding psychiatric disorders related to cancer and addiction. However, there is a vast number of directions in which psilocybin research can go as it appears to be a versatile substance with multifaceted therapeutic properties.

Depression is one of the most deeply researched conditions in relation to using psilocybin therapy. Not long ago, the FDA gave the research of psilocybin therapy a breakthrough therapy designation, which can also be translated as a "review fast track" for the treatment of depression. Psilocybin research began with pilot trials, and there have also been more varied phase II and phase III trials, all approved by the FDA. An example is a phase III trial being planned at the Usona Institute, which is also a research center for psychedelics. This trial is expected to provide solid results regarding the use of psilocybin and its effectiveness in treating depression.

In the case of addictions and addictive behavior, a pilot study was conducted at John Hopkins University. The study was led by Dr. Matthew Johnson, an associate professor in behavioral sciences and psychiatry at the Johns Hopkins School of Medicine. This study found that using psilocybin therapy can cause a significant reduction in smoking cravings and improve abstinence from smoking within the study's 12 month follow-up period. Johnson is also confident that psilocybin has similar therapeutic potential when it comes to cocaine addiction and alcohol addiction.

Dr. Matthew Johnson explains this by identifying addictive behaviors as a "narrowed mental and behavioral repertoire" (Mammoser, 2019). During treatment, psilocybin shakes the individual out of their addictive mental routines and can create mental plasticity that allows them to see the bigger picture by not being attached to or part of it. This is supported by a smaller open-label study that also focused on psilocybin therapy with specifically alcohol addiction. The study found that treatment had a positive effect on both heavy drinking and, although less so, habitual drinking as well. Trials focusing on cocaine addiction are currently being conducted in Alabama.

Cancer-related psychological disorders include high levels of existential stress when patients know that their life is ending soon due to their terminal illness. In these cases, psilocybin has also been used therapeutically, and according to Dr. Charles Grob, a professor in psychiatry from the David Geffen School of Medicine at UCLA, the preliminary trial results indicated some promising results. The *Journal of Psychopharmacology* published a research report about two smaller studies where magic mushrooms were administered to cancer patients. Some of these advanced cancer patients described the feeling they experience after treatment as a cloud of doom that they felt lifting. Grob's first study was a pilot study conducted in 2011, which also focused on the same existentially motivated mental distress cancer patients experience when being diagnosed with an advanced stage of cancer or terminal cancer (Mammoser, 2019).

Big Pharma and the Banning of Magic Mushrooms

Like most psychedelic substances, psilocybin is also classified as Schedule 1 in the United States. Although this seems to some to be a sinister decision by Big Pharma, or a conspiracy to keep psilocybin off the market and banned for medicinal use, there are researchers and advocates for the use of psilocybin that agree that making the hallucinogenic freely available, or even available in the form of a prescription, is dangerous to some patients' health. Shortly, we'll get into more specific details on this.

The decision to make psilocybin a Schedule I substance was made in 1971 by the DEA's Controlled Substances Act. The decision is based on it not being deemed safe even under medical supervision, having a high potential for abuse, and when the banning was officiated, there was no medical evidence that supported accepted medical use of the substance in the United States. You might find this similar to why MDMA was officially classified as a Schedule I substance.

However, as recently as 2010, a movement to legalize magic mushrooms started forming in Denver, Colorado. Colorado later became the first state to decriminalize psilocybin in May 2019 (Kenney, 2019). In November 2020, Measure 109 was passed in the state of Oregon, which legalizes the use of psilocybin for individuals that are above the age of 21. After another official voting, the substance was officially decriminalized. The reason for the decriminalization of psilocybin is due to researchers promoting its relevance and therapeutic properties for the treatment of PTSD, anxiety, and depression, to name a few. Measure 109 has not been enacted yet, and this will only happen after the completion of a developmental stage, which is predicted to last about two years. Washington, DC also followed suit and decriminalized psilocybin in November 2020.

Currently, psilocybin is not available to any medical professional in a clinical setting as it is still classified as a Schedule I substance or drug. For research purposes, obtaining the substance requires a waiver from the FDA. For psilocybin to be used in therapy or legally prescribed to patients, its classification needs to change from Schedule I to Schedule II. (Drugs.com, 2021).

The Legal Status of Psilocybin in Different Countries

- In Mexico, the possession of mushrooms containing psilocybin is illegal. Although, there will be no legal enforcement if these mushrooms are grown by, or belong to, indigenous cultures. The cultivation of mushrooms that contain psilocybin is illegal unless the mushrooms are grown in the wild. The sale and transport of these mushrooms are also illegal.

- In Austria, it's illegal to transport and sell magic mushrooms. Possession of magic mushrooms has been decriminalized, and the cultivation thereof is also legal as long as the mushrooms are not grown or cultivated for consumption. Individuals caught possessing mushrooms intended for personal use may be required to undergo free therapy.

- Since 2018, magic mushrooms have been illegal in Vietnam.

- In the Netherlands, magic mushrooms are only legal in the form of truffles.

- Although Spain decriminalized consumption and personal possession of magic mushrooms, psilocybin as a substance is still illegal. Cultivation and the sale of magic mushrooms are also illegal, but the legality regarding grow kits and spores is a bit vague.

- Possession, cultivation, sale, and transport of magic mushrooms are all legal in Jamaica. Jamaica sells magic mushrooms openly.

- In Brazil, it is legal to cultivate, possess, transport, and sell, psilocybin mushrooms. Psilocin and psilocybin as pure substances are listed as illegal, however, the mushrooms themselves are not seen as illegal.

- In Portugal, magic mushrooms are decriminalized but still illegal. If someone is caught with any amount intended for personal use, they may be required to go for therapy or rehabilitation.

- The British Virgin Islands allow the cultivation and possession of magic mushrooms. It is, however, illegal (but unenforced) to transport or sell the mushrooms.

- Magic mushrooms are legal in Samoa.

- Wanting to be consistent with UN Policy, psilocybin is not legal in Italy. However, magic mushrooms are decriminalized. Grow kits and spores are legal for selling and obtaining, but there are administrative punishments, like losing one's driver's license for getting caught with the mushrooms.

- Canada is one of the few countries that allows the possession and consumption of psychedelic mushrooms to individuals who suffer from depression or other mental conditions. Psilocybin and psilocin are illegal to obtain, produce, or possess without a prescription or a license as the substance is classified as schedule III under the Controlled Drugs and Substances Act. There are, however, online dispensaries that exist that openly sell microdoses to Canadian patients who have medical prescriptions (News 18, 2020).

Magic Mushrooms Today

Due to the fact that these substances are still being tested, and some are in preliminary trials, it is important to consider one's own health—especially mental health—when using psychedelic substances recreationally. Always keep in mind that, not being a researcher or an expert, moderation is key.

The Risks of Experimenting With Psilocybin Without Supervision

Although prohibited, psilocybin is available to the public if they know where to find it. The substance is used recreationally and is often mixed with other substances like marijuana, alcohol, or even laced with LSD. Many people used magic mushrooms during the counterculture movement and experimented with them by combining them with other hallucinogenic drugs. However, what are the risks, and what are you doing to your body if you consume these substances without fully knowing what they are and what they can do to you?

Your body can develop an increased level of tolerance to psilocybin, depending on how much you take and how often you take it. With regular use, psilocybin tolerance will develop quickly, and you will need to consume larger doses to get the desired effect. High tolerance is dangerous for your health—an overdose of psilocybin can lead to serious health issues, though, it is not fatal (Hartney, 2012).

The recreational use of psilocybin is not currently legal in most parts of the United States and other countries, as it is not safe to take the substance without professional assistance or advice. If psilocybin is used incorrectly on a long-term basis, it can have drastic effects on an individual's health including extended or long-term changes to their personality and the experience of flashbacks long after the substance is out of their system.

A pharmaceutical company that tested a sample of mushrooms that were purchased also revealed some shocking information. Only a small percentage of these mushrooms were actually real "magic mushrooms." The analysis indicated that 31% of the mushrooms were normal mushrooms you can buy at your local grocery store but laced with LSD, 37% were just normal mushrooms that had no hallucinogenic properties at all, and only 28% of these mushrooms contained inherent hallucinogenic properties (Hartney, 2012).

Although psilocybin is proven to be safe for the treatment of some conditions, there are some myths when it comes to its recreational use. For example, because magic mushrooms are not as potent as LSD, recreational drug users tend to think that their trip on shrooms is safer because shrooms are milder. It might depend on the dose you decide to take, but really, this is a complete myth. If you don't have any scientific knowledge of these substances and how they affect the brain, then making an assumption like this can be incredibly dangerous. It is a fact that psilocybin also causes "bad trips," which can be terrifying to the individual experiencing it, and can lead to subsequent anxiety, despite its reputation for being a mild drug. It is also easy to confuse mushrooms that contain psilocybin with mushrooms called "fly agaric mushrooms," which contain a different hallucinogenic compound that causes a less pleasant experience. These mushrooms will make you drool, twitch, vomit, sweat, and you may even become completely delirious.

These side-effects will not come from the therapeutic use of psilocybin but rather from its recreational use. Psilocybin is another misunderstood substance that can actually affect the brain's plasticity and subsequently influence addictive behaviors and change people's lives—people who suffer from a variety of conditions and experience unnecessary pain. There is still much work to be done in order to get psilocybin any form of approval or legalization, but the research to back it up already exists and is constantly evolving (Palmer, 2016).

Thomas Chan: I am God

One example of an individual who ingested psilocybin and experienced a "bad trip" that went horribly wrong happened in the life of Thomas Chan. Chan was convicted of manslaughter in December 2018 in Peterborough, Canada, for killing his father, Dr. Andrew Chan, who worked as a gastroenterologist. During the same episode, Thomas Chan also permanently maimed his father's girlfriend, Lynn Witteveen, at his father's home on December 28th, 2015. Chan's father had cameras installed around the house, and according to footage taken from these cameras, Chan entered his father's home on December 28. He found his father in the kitchen, and while repeatedly screaming, "I am God," he attacked his father with a kitchen knife. His father can be heard trying to bring him back to his senses by saying, "Thomas—it's Daddy, it's Daddy."

Thomas proceeded to the bedroom where he found his father's girlfriend, Lynn Witteveen, and stabbed her multiple times as well. Lynn survived the attack. Both of these violent acts occurred while Thomas Chan was under the influence of magic mushrooms. Chan told the police that he felt he was turning his life around after attempting to do so for some time when he suddenly had this violent episode that ended up ruining his life completely. He claims to suffer from severe anxiety and depression which is a result of suffering multiple concussions when playing rugby as a teenager—this is why he was taking psilocybin. Chan's attorneys wanted to argue that the main legal question should not be whether he committed the acts, but rather, whether he really is criminally liable for them (The Peterborough Examiner, 2020; Deeth, 2020).

Chan's use of psilocybin to treat his conditions appears to be fuelled by misinformation regarding the therapeutic use of this psychedelic substance. He recalls reading *The Third Eye,* meditating under the influence of psilocybin, and starting to hallucinate that he was God. He said that he thought he was God, but he felt that everything was against him. According to Chan, it all "went South" from there. This method of self-dosing leans towards the "Timothy Leary" recreational and spiritual psychedelic dogma. The toxicologist, Daryl Mayers also said that it is very unlikely that others would have the same reaction if they were to ingest the same mushrooms. This is also true in Chan's situation; no one else who took the mushrooms with him had any violent reactions or hallucinations that reached that level. Thus, it shows that Chan was the minority in the group and experienced an abnormal reaction to the mushrooms. It is speculated that this could be because he also suffers from mental health issues due to multiple previous concussions.

Although the psilocybin may have played a role in Chan killing his father and almost killing his father's girlfriend, this is a fringe case, and it cannot be used to prove that using or ingesting psilocybin is a life-threatening substance. It was used by a boy who already had neural abnormalities and he should have been advised by a medical practitioner (if this did not already occur). This is regardless of whether the mushrooms may potentially have been laced with another substance which would likely have triggered his violent behavior. A doctor could have alerted him to stay away from mind-altering substances when he himself did not understand the risks of his mental condition when taking psilocybin (The Peterborough Examiner, 2020; Deeth, 2020).

COMPASS Pathways and the Study of Psilocybin

COMPASS is a company focusing on mental healthcare that aims to bring access to new and innovative treatment solutions for mental health patients. COMPASS received what was seen as a "breakthrough therapy designation" by the FDA to research and test a psilocybin-based drug for the treatment of mental health issues. The FDA approval was granted in August 2018 (Lynch, 2019).

Even though these studies show amazing results that can help so many people improve their quality of life, there is still a reluctance to legalize psilocybin because administering an incorrect dose can lead to adverse effects and, ironically, psychological issues. George Greer is very firm about the conditions of legalizing psilocybin. He notes that, if it is to be legalized, it cannot be freely available to the public, and should ideally be administered in a controlled environment by therapists and medical professionals specializing in this type of therapy. Handing out a prescription and allowing the patient to take home a large supply of the substance can be extremely dangerous. Why is Greer so firm on this point? There are lots of medications that can cause harm if taken in doses that exceed that which is prescribed. Simply put, because psilocybin gives one that feeling of escape, a patient may be more likely to abuse their freedom with this substance. Additionally, there are major downsides to taking too much psilocybin:

- Taking a misinformed dosage of psilocybin can cause irregular heartbeat and increased blood pressure.

- The substance is extremely dangerous for those who have experienced episodes of psychosis or mania, which includes individuals with Bipolar Disorder and Schizophrenia. Psilocybin can trigger such an episode, and as individuals who suffer from these conditions may know, such an episode can be life-altering in an adverse way.

- There are rare accounts of individuals experiencing what is called "bad trips," which have ended in their committing suicide while they are under the influence of the hallucinogenic substance.

- Other effects of psilocybin that can occur because of its effect on the neurotransmitter, serotonin, are related to sexual behavior, muscle control, sensory perception, one's mood, sleep cycles or quality, body temperature, and appetite (Drugs. com, 2021; Mammoser, 2019).

Microdosing With Psilocybin

Microdosing has become a common practice with psilocybin and its psychedelic cousins like MDMA and LSD. Chances are that when you microdose, you will not have another billion-dollar epiphany to the likes of Steve Jobs; however, individuals who practice microdosing, especially with psilocybin, say that the quality of their lives has dramatically improved. The definition of microdosing is the consumption of tiny doses of a substance on a regular basis. By "regular basis," we are referring to once every second day, as is most commonly practiced.

Microdosing started gaining a reputation since it's a popular practice among the rich and famous; however, there are those who wonder whether there are any real health benefits behind this practice or how it can improve your life. Early reviews and studies about microdosing do suggest that the outcome is in the individual's favor as taking such a small dosage of psilocybin will not put you on a trip, but it can enhance important components of your everyday life, like your overall work performance, your ability to think creatively, your level of efficiency when conducting everyday tasks, the improvement of pain relief, and soothing of symptoms of depression without you having to go on a trip every day. However, these are the outcomes based on literature from surveys. The results from clinical trials will be able to provide more concrete evidence about how efficient microdosing really is (Siebert, 2020).

Dosage-wise, one needs to take about one-tenth of a trip-inducing dosage of psilocybin. That is if you are content with not meeting the gods, experiencing a sacred journey, or suddenly understanding the hidden wisdom of time and space. A study conducted in the Netherlands at the University of Leiden and published in 2018, reported that microdosing with psilocybin has clear and noticeable effects on mental abilities, like problem-solving and rational thinking, and that microdosing can even make abstract thinking and reasoning more accessible for an individual. Apart from these noticeable improvements, individuals who practice microdosing also appear to have a more stimulated sense of creative thinking. Bernard Hommel, who led the study, also noted that there was a notable improvement in participants' divergent and convergent thinking abilities. Divergent thinking involves mental flexibility, and convergent thinking involves one's ability to focus on abstract concepts while also having the ability to find a single solution for a well-explained or defined problem. Most psychologists would agree that both types of thinking are essential for productive levels of creativity (Begley, 2018).

After conducting this test, researchers came to the conclusion that microdosing with psilocybin sharpens the individual's senses, making them slightly more conscious as if their energy fields and atoms are raised just a tiny bit. This is enough to make any scientist excited, so they continued with another organized research study. They took a logical first step by zooming in on the most common elevated experiences reported by the participants; these included cognitive flexibility, a heightened sense of creativity, and improved problem-solving. In 2018, the University of Leiden's Luisa Prochazkova led this study and recruited 38 voluntary participants from the *Psychedelic Society of the Netherlands*.

Because the researchers had some valuable background information from the previous study, they started this second study by first evaluating the participants through three standard psychological tests. These tests were taken by the participants before they were administered a microdose of psilocybin. The first and second tests were about creative problem-solving, and the third test assessed their fluid intelligence. To make sure that the research was based on completely accurate doses of psilocybin, the mushroom samples were tested. Carefully calculating their dose from a "normal trip" dose, which is about 3 grams of psilocybin, they needed a microdose of 0.33 grams for each participant. Ultimately, the dosage consumed by participants averaged 0.37 grams of psilocybin. After administering the micro dose to each participant, a

90-minute waiting period was applied before the tests were taken again (Begley, 2018).

The first assessment, testing creativity, was a Picture Concept test, where participants were shown three rows of three pictures. They had to choose three pictures, one from each row, that they thought were most closely related. This means that the brain needs to practice convergent thinking by considering alternatives, linking related objects, and dismissing those that are deemed unrelated.

The next test was called an Alternative Uses test. In this assessment, the participants were given five minutes to think of different ways to use an object, for example, a towel or a pencil. The task required divergent thinking as the participants needed to find new associations for the object not linked to its traditional function.

The final test was called a Progressive Matrices test. This test assessed the participants' fluid intelligence by giving them blocks of three-by-three or two-by-two to look at with the bottom right block missing. The participants then had to look at six alternative blocks and decide which option was the best fit for the blank space.

After assessing both the pre-and-post microdose tests from each participant, the researchers found that no participant had a significantly higher score in the Progressive Matrices test. When looking at the results of the Alternative Uses test, there was a significant improvement, and participants were much more creative in their newly found uses for pencils and towels. The Picture Concept test also showed a notable improvement, which indicated a heightened ability for convergent thinking. These fascinating results led the researchers to conclude that microdosing with psilocybin can allow individuals to think out of the box and develop higher-level creative concepts and ideas. It does not, however, appear to have an effect on fluid intelligence.

One point of criticism that can be mentioned regarding the methodology of this research study is that the participants were given the same tests twice, which meant that it was not necessarily only the effect of the psilocybin that caused the improvement in the second test but could have due to a familiarity with them. This, however, still doesn't explain why there was only a significant improvement in the two creativity-prospecting tests while the fluid intelligence test results remained relatively the same (Begley, 2018).

In February 2020, a research study was published in the medical journal *Psychopharmacology* about microdosing and its effects. This study was largely based on a global survey, and the hypotheses that required an answer asked whether microdosing can improve an individual's mental health and also possibly help with substance abuse-related disorders and addiction, for which psilocybin's effects are famous. Because the study relied on a survey, there was a variety of information that landed in the hands of researchers. For example, 21% of the participants were microdosing to ease symptoms of depression, 2% were microdosing to help with substance abuse, 7% indicated that they were self-medicating for anxiety, and 9% stated other mental health-related reasons. Subsequently, 44% of these individuals reported a significant improvement in their mental health through microdosing, and 50% reported that they were able to stop taking antidepressants. 1.3% reported that microdosing worsened their condition and 9% reported that they didn't experience any difference during the process (Siebert, 2020).

The benefits of microdosing were also evident in the 2019 Global Drug Survey as they added a subsection about microdosing for participants to answer. Almost 7,000 participants reported the use of psychedelics, and the subsequent report that was also published in *Psychopharmacology* indicated that the pros of microdosing by far outweigh the cons.

Chapter 2: The Magic in Magic Mushrooms

Dosage Guide

Level					
Lvl 1: Microdose	Lvl 2: Mini Dose	Lvl 3: Museum Dose	Lvl 4: Moderate Dose	Lvl 5: Mega Dose	Lvl 6: The Dose of the Hero
Dose					
0.05mg - 0.25 mg	0.25 mg - 0.75 mg	0.5g - 1.5g	2.0g - 3.5g	3.5g - 5g	5grams +
Effects					
Increased Mental Stamina →		Enhanced Concentration →		Uplifted Mood	
Altered Perception of Sound →	Anomalies of the Short-term Memory →		Enhanced Visuals →	Mild Euphoria →	Feeling "stoned"
Colors become vivid →	Open and Closed Eye Visuals →		Distracted Patterns of Thought →		An Enhanced Level of Creativity
Kaleidoscopic Visions →	Warped Visions →	Mild Hallucinations →	3 Dimensional Closed-Eye Visions →	Minor Synesthesia →	A Distorted Sense of Time
Full-blown Hallucinations →	Dissolution of the Ego →	A Mild Disconnect from Reality →	No Sense of Time →	Synesthesia →	Out of Body Experiences
A Complete Alteration of the Senses →		Ego Death →		A Total Disconnect from Reality	

(Reality Sandwich, 2019a)

Chapter 3:
Stigmatized Acid

LSD and psilocybin were, and are still often, associated with each other because they are used in similar medical and scientific trials. LSD had a similar origin due to also containing natural psychedelic components in its make-up, as opposed to being strictly created in a lab. An extensive research history reveals LSD to be more than just the recreational drug it is most commonly known as. It also has a spectacular political history and is most likely one of the most demonized psychedelic drugs in existence today. There are two very different sides to the coin that represents LSD.

What is LSD?

The generic name for LSD is Lysergic acid diethylamide; however, if you want to know what you're talking about, then you can also familiarize yourself with the more than 80 other names that have developed on the streets. The most well-known name for LSD is acid, but you can also call it *Doses Blotter, Dots, Mellow Yellow, Trips, Window Pane*, or even the names reflected on blotter paper designs, such as *Purple Dragon*. Synthesized for the first time in 1938, LSD is considered to be a very potent substance. LSD itself is made synthetically from a natural compound called lysergic acid that is found in a fungus called ergot. This specific fungus is known to grow on grains, specifically on rye.

Whereas with other psychedelics a "trip dose" will likely be in grams, a few micrograms of acid is enough to put you on a full-blown trip.

If you buy LSD on the street, you'll find it in different forms and administered in different ways. A few examples include: being in the form of gelatin that is cut in thin squares and are known as window panes; being in a tablet form or capsules (the tablets are tiny and known as 'microdots'); being in a liquid form or in the form of sugar cubes; being in a pure liquid form; and finally, being in the form of blotter paper, which is an absorbent type of paper soaked in LSD and cut into small squares. The last manifestation of LSD described above is the most commonly available one and is also, as previously mentioned, the source of one of its names.

LSD itself takes on a crystalline structure. To dilute it, it is mixed with other inactive components to form an odorless and colorless liquid that is described to have a faintly bitter aftertaste. Depending on its form, LSD can be injected, snorted, or even inhaled. Although there is no known dosage of LSD that is lethal, death has occurred due to injuries sustained while under the influence of large doses of LSD (Drugs.com, 2014).

History and Traditional Use
Ergot on Rye and the Salem Witch Trials

LSD, as earlier described, comes from a fungus—ergot—that grows on grains and carries the psychedelic component that translates over to its synthesized form, acid. If grains that contain ergot are consumed, the individual who consumed these grains may suffer several severe effects from this potent hallucinogenic fungus. This happened several hundred years ago in the Puritan village of Salem, Massachusetts, where a sudden and unexpected wave of witchcraft accusations overcame the small town. These accusations were triggered by the strange behavior of two girls named Abigail Williams and Betty Paris, who exhibited strange behavioral and physical symptoms, which included convulsing. They were subsequently diagnosed by the local doctor as being bewitched. Not long after the doctor's diagnosis, other townspeople started to show similar symptoms and behavior, which spooked the townspeople and triggered a massive witch hunt and led to the famous Salem Witch Trials. After the trials ended in May 1693, one person had been crushed to death by stones, nineteen people had been hanged, and four died in prison. All of these individuals were accused of being witches. Some believe that these individuals were persecuted because they were really witches, but others have a more scientific approach and theory in mind.

A new and more logical theory came from Dr. Linnda Caporael in 1976. Caporael, who is from the Rensselaer Polytechnic Institute, conducted research on this event, and hypothesized that the townspeople of Salem were not bewitched at all; in fact, they most likely suffered from ergotism, a disease contracted when consuming rye contaminated by ergot. After the fungus starts to grow in the rye, it begins to flourish, and replaces the shoots of rye with what is called ergot sclerotia. These purplish-black growths contain ergotamine and lysergic acid, and the rye was most likely eaten in large quantities by the Salem townspeople as it may have been a staple food. Her theory drew the attention of many historians as it made sense contextually. The development of the ergot on the rye was very likely due to weather conditions as, around the same time as the trials, the town of Salem experienced an unusually cold winter and a very dewy spring, which presented the perfect conditions for the development of the fungi on damp, rotting rye.

Ergotism, which is subsequently contracted from the consumption of the ergot sclerotia, is also known as St. Anthony's Fire. Common symptoms include severe muscular spasms, convulsions, delusions, sensations of organisms crawling under one's skin, hallucinations, and in the most severe cases, gangrene can develop on an individual's extremities. What happened in Salem was also called the Salem Witch Trials because those who were most affected were younger women and girls, who, according to experts and historians, would have had the weakest and, most likely, not fully developed immune systems. This factor would have made them far more susceptible to developing severe cases of ergotism, which would cause them to exhibit the sinister symptoms that would make them appear bewitched. Lacking the scientific knowledge of the possibility that a fungus growing on their grains could potentially be the cause of the presenting symptoms, the doctor's diagnosis of bewitchment was accepted and the rest, as they say, is history (Lohnes, 2019).

CHAPTER 2: THE MAGIC IN MAGIC MUSHROOMS

The Discovery of LSD

LSD was formally discovered in 1938 by Swiss chemist Albert Hoffman for the purpose of stopping postpartum bleeding or hemorrhage. Hoffman was also the first individual to experience LSD's psychedelic properties after he accidentally came into contact with the substance himself. This happened five years after its discovery, in 1943, when he accidentally ingested a very small amount of the substance and subsequently saw amazing shapes and a kaleidoscope of colors. Three days after Hoffman's mini-trip, he took a larger dose of the drug. It was April 9th, 1943, and he was riding his bicycle home from work as he was not able to use a car due to restrictions put in place by WWII. This day is still celebrated by many recreational LSD users as the 'Bicycle Day" (History.com Editors, 2018). These effects immediately drew a significant amount of interest to the potential of the substance, and only a decade after its founding, at the end of the 1940s, psychiatrists were talking about the possible therapeutic effects of LSD. LSD was even manufactured, marketed, and distributed by the Big Pharma company Sandoz. It was branded under the name "Delysid," and in the 1950s, it was used in psychiatry in the United States and Europe (Fuentes et al., 2020).

During the earlier years of experimenting and investigating LSD, scientists classified it as a psychomimetic drug, and not a psychedelic drug, due to the fact that they believed it mimicked mental illness after ingestion. An example of one of these mental illnesses scientists thought LSD mimicked was Schizophrenia, because of the near-psychotic and hallucinatory experience this drug causes. Doctors who worked with LSD and administered it to their patients during the 1950s had also taken the substance at least once to understand what their patients were experiencing when under the influence. At first, medical professionals tried to use LSD to find out more about mental illness, which they found was not very successful. They would administer the patient with LSD and record the session. The patient would be monitored with different types of machines and would have to undergo intelligence and psychological testing.

Administering LSD to a mentally ill individual, especially a dose that would not be considered a microdose, can exacerbate the individual's mental condition as the drug causes hallucinations where one would see vivid colors and images, clear sounds that sound almost too real, a sense of detachment from oneself, a distorted sense of space and time, all types of patterns moving about, and even the existential feeling of being incomplete. Now, if you can imagine administering this substance to a schizophrenic patient for testing and the absolute horror they would experience, such a person would never be the same again. LSD does not have this extremely negative effect on everyone, however. Still, due to the medical community's focus on mental illness and their likening the experience caused by LSD to that of Schizophrenia, the public was very much appalled at the idea of such a substance.

LSD, the CIA, and Mind Control

The CIA had become increasingly interested in experimenting with mind control as part of their Cold War agenda. The CIA's then-newly appointed director, Allan Dulles, implemented Project MK-Ultra, which would be a top-secret broad-spectrum human experiment that focused on the undercover use of chemical and biological materials. MK-Ultra included mind-control experiments that focused on how substances like LSD can modify a person's behavior. The tools used in these experiments included drugs, electric shock therapy, toxins, hypnosis, polygraphs, and radiation.

They relied on test subjects to conduct their experiments. The subjects were either volunteers who freely offered themselves for experimentation, volunteers who eventually agreed due to some persuasion or intimidation, and individuals who had no idea that they were part of this program. Examples of the variety of test subjects recruited by these means include mentally impaired children, patients from state mental hospitals, and American soldiers. The CIA also used prisoners and got their consent by offering shorter sentences or extended recreational time.

During the 1940s, a little bird told the CIA that the Soviet Union was producing large amounts of LSD and that they were at an advanced stage in their study of the substance as a weapon for war. This gave the

CIA a huge fright because, at that point, they did not know a lot about acid and its effects. A CIA officer admitted that the organization had never considered the potential of this substance on the human mind if used in an abusive or improper manner. They consequently attempted to purchase all LSD supplies they could get their hands on, and the status quo swiftly changed as they started their own research projects.

In 1953 on November 18th, ten scientists met for discussions in a remote cabin located in the Maryland forests. They came to a consensus that if the drug LSD is to be understood thoroughly, they would have to conduct an uninformed experiment. One prisoner and ex-crime boss, Whitey Bulger, tells about his experiences after being injected with LSD. He was one of the test subjects for the MK-Ultra project. Whitey recalls completely losing his appetite, experiencing the room changing into different shapes, experiencing feelings of paranoia, having violent impulses, and seeing blood oozing out of the walls. He also recalls seeing a camera changing into the head of a dog and people turning suddenly into skeletons when he looked at them (Nofil, 2019).

The CIA's interest became focused on LSD and its mind-altering effects as part of their "brain warfare" operation, and they were interested in how the substance could be used to effectively interrogate the enemy, among other harrowing ideas. As MK-Ultra became a reality, the CIA made a shift in their position towards LSD from defensive to offensive. LSD would be administered to unsuspecting citizens. If they could, they would find volunteers, and they even administered the drug to fellow CIA employees by putting it in their drinks. The CIA's experimentation with LSD became more and more detailed, and an example of such an experiment is Operation Midnight Climax.

Operation Midnight Climax was one of the CIA's most elaborate attempts to observe the spontaneous effects of LSD. They recruited George White from the Federal Bureau of Narcotics and proceeded to decorate a bedroom bordello-style in a building on 225 Chestnut Street in 1955. An engineering student from Berkeley was hired to bug the room and install a two-way mirror so White could sit behind the wall and observe the goings-on inside unnoticed. Sex workers were hired by the CIA to lure unsuspecting 'clients' into the room and give them LSD. Then, White could sit and watch how the drug manifested in terms of behavior on the unsuspecting victim. The sex workers received small cash payments accompanied by a promise that they will not be hustled by law enforcement (Nofil, 2019).

After observing these sexual encounters for a while, the CIA came up with a new idea—using sex and LSD as a weapon to extract secrets from the enemy and training sex workers to act as confidential informants, learning state secrets to take back to the Central Intelligence Agency. They eventually concluded that the most advantageous timing to extract confidential information from a suspect is as soon as possible after they've had sex with the prostitute.

Of course, the CIA's MK-Ultra operations inevitably had to come to an end, and they pushed their LSD-fuelled experiments up to 1963, where it ended in a slump. A member of the Director General's office caught wind of the CIA's use of involuntary subjects. Despite the MK-Ultra director's objections, they were forced to follow new ethical guidelines that prohibited this practice. Thus, according to what we know, all testing and research that involves non-consenting subjects then came to an abrupt end (Nofil, 2019).

Some of the most disturbing details of the CIA's LSD research came to light during the congressional hearings held in 1977. These hearings were overseen by Senator Edward Kennedy, and many ex-CIA employees were brought in for questioning regarding the MK-Ultra operation and the CIA's experiments with LSD. These ex-employees were interrogated about the criteria used to identify subjects or participants, the individuals who oversaw these programs' operations, and whether any of these programs are still active. One disturbing detail that surfaced from this congressional hearing is the suicide of an Army scientist named Frank Olson who, in 1953, jumped from his hotel window to his death a few days after consuming a drink spiked with LSD.

It is safe to say that the extent the CIA went to in their secret operations was due to the fact that they had no idea what the Soviets were capable of; they only knew that the Soviets were experimenting with mind-altering weapons. Nevertheless, they knew very well that what they were doing was unethical, as demonstrated in this quote:

"The knowledge that the Agency is engaging in unethical and illicit activities would have serious repercussions in political and diplomatic circles, and would be detrimental to the accomplishment of its mission." (Nofil, 2019).

Many of the employees who were brought in for interrogation testified that they had little to no recollection of these experiments, and after an investigation, it was also established that all documentation of this operation had been destroyed.

Studies and Interesting Findings

One of the biggest foes standing in the way toward LSD gaining credibility is its bad reputation. However, it is not the drug itself that deserves that reputation but the individuals and institutions that misused it. Scientists have remained curious about this substance and whether it has any therapeutic potential, and after some decades that served as a cool-off period, research is getting back into gear. Here are some of the most interesting recent findings:

The Contribution of Dr. Sidney Cohen

If there's someone worth mentioning for giving LSD the credit it deserves, one of these individuals is definitely Dr. Sidney Cohen. As a professor in clinical pharmacology, his bread and butter was studying all types of illnesses and drugs. This meant that his path would inevitably cross with LSD and its bad reputation, and luckily it did. He started taking LSD himself in 1955, and his expectations, as dictated by the majority opinion of the drug, were proven to be incorrect. Instead, he had an experience that he described as his frustrations disappearing and finding himself in a heavenly and majestic place. Cohen was bowled over by this experience, and it inspired him to dig deeper.

Hereafter, Cohen started conducting his own experiments and developed a methodology different from the mainstream approach followed by researchers. What Cohen wanted to achieve was to define the effect of LSD as a "shift of consciousness." This phrase essentially means that, instead of focusing on paranoia, the effects of LSD as a therapeutic tool can help an individual transcend the humdrum of their everyday life and the shackles of their egos. Cohen was not alone in this belief as it was also shared by the famous author, Aldous Huxley, who wrote one of the most renowned counterculture works, *The Doors of Perception*.

A year later, in 1956, Cohen was experimenting with LSD as a treatment for depression and alcoholism through psychotherapy. LSD was administered to individuals for a period of about a year, and specific points were monitored, like whether the subject's affinity for alcohol lessened, whether they could maintain stable relationships, and whether they could keep a steady job. In order to support the research, LSD was endorsed by Bill Wilson, the founder of Alcoholics Anonymous. Bill Wilson himself tried LSD along with his colleague, Betty Eisner, and he was so impressed that he started his own private LSD get-together in New York City. It is important to note that the participants that Cohen used for his experiments did not have severe mental illnesses and that their conditions can rather be described as 'minor.'

Cohen later joined forces with other researchers, like Oscar Janiger, to further expand their studies on LSD—this time zooming in on the drug's ability to enhance creativity in the brain. Although these experiments did not turn out to be conclusive or have concrete results, the fact that their findings were made public did influence individuals like Timothy Leary, and others, like Richard Alpert, to look at LSD for recreational use. Cohen, however, did not support this idea, and in the end, Cohen became opposed to LSD entirely and the way it was—and still is—loosely used; however, he still made a massive contribution to understanding the potential of the drug (DiPaolo, 2018).

Studies on LSD and Behavioral Patterns

Recent studies indicate that psychedelic drugs like LSD can actually promote the growth of neurons in the brain, which affects the brain's structure in a good way. In the case of LSD, the neurotransmitters it had a notable effect on are both serotonin and dopamine. Current research explores how LSD may be able to 'reset' certain neural pathways in the brain to, very much like psilocybin, get rid of bad habits, and encourage new ways of thinking and approaching situations in life (Alcohol and Drug Foundation, 2018).

A 2016 study conducted in London showed that LSD can affect and change deeply embedded thought patterns that lead to behavioral patterns. The study was conducted on individuals with no history of mental illness. They were given a single dose of LSD, and after a two-week period, the participants reported feeling more optimistic with a sense of openness and elevated mood. Another earlier trial that was conducted on patients who faced either a terminal or life-threatening disease concluded that the administration of LSD to these patients dramatically improved their existential anxiety that was related to the anticipation of death. The mental improvement in these patients included showing increased mental strength, feeling more relaxed, and feeling more self-assured despite their diagnoses. Although researchers have witnessed these outcomes after conducting LSD-related studies, they are not entirely sure how the processing of the psychedelic in the body affects the brain in order to bring about these positive results. After all, this same substance can also cause adverse and tragically negative results in the same person if a different dose were taken.

Questions that sprang from these specific studies included how long patients need to be treated with LSD before the treatment is not required anymore. The results of LSD-assisted therapy, which is always conducted at a clinic and under the supervision of a medical professional, have shown to have speedy results—but how long do they last? Another question that is yet to be answered is whether LSD can be used for the treatment of individuals with mental disorders or mental illnesses. The only adverse effects currently recorded from these studies is that some participants experience confusion and anxiety post-consumption; and in very rare cases, self-harm has occurred that was not part of the therapeutic context. For these reasons, all research and testing remain supervised, participants are thoroughly informed before the process begins, and administration of LSD always occurs within a controlled environment (Alcohol and Drug Foundation, 2018).

LSD Studies Focused on Autism and Social Anxiety

LSD, as we know, has been experimented with in many ways—some of which have been highly unethical. And because of its negative associations, the only thing gained from all of these past studies is a sense of notoriety and stigma. In past studies, scientists could not determine how LSD works and how it affects the brain's processes and functioning. McGill University in Canada launched a research study that focuses on LSD and its effect on one's ability to socially interact. This study was subsequently published in the scientific journal *PNAS*. In the study, the researchers administered a low dose of LSD to mice for seven days and discovered that there is a notable increase in these animals' sociability. It is important to note that the brain of a mouse does not work in the exact same way as a human brain, but with mice, they were able to identify the underlying mechanism that causes the behavioral effect. Researchers subsequently discovered that LSD has the ability to activate the *AMPHA* receptors and the *5-HT2A* serotonin receptors, which are both required to work together to create the ability of social interaction

What makes the above-mentioned research a breakthrough is not the knowledge that LSD can bind with the *5-HT2A* serotonin receptors, but that the prosocial element in LSD specifically causes a chain reaction when first activating the *5-HT2A* serotonin receptors. This activation subsequently causes the activation with the *AMPHA* receptors and the protein complex *mTORC1*. It is this sequence of activations that increases sociability. These receptors and proteins are part of dysregulated pathways (which control our emotional responses) in an individual's brain suffering from mental disorders that include antisocial symptoms, or "social deficits," like autism spectrum disorder and severe social anxiety.

Researchers at McGill University hope to eventually implement studies where they can explore whether microdosing with LSD on humans with these social or behavioral deficits can be proven as a safe and successful therapeutic approach that makes a difference in these individuals' lives. Dr. Gabriella Gobbi, a professor in psychiatry, also at McGill University, adds that being able to interact socially is a fundamental component of being human and of human behavior. Researchers now know that psychedelic compounds like LSD can open up these social pathways and increase social behavior in an individual, which means that they may also be a great help in developing new and safe psychiatric drugs or treatments in the future (Martin, 2021).

A Groundbreaking Neurological Study on LSD and Brain Activity

One of the most mind-boggling findings from a neurological study using LSD is that LSD actually frees brain activity from its anatomical shackles. That in itself sounds like something that can only happen on a psychedelic trip, as brain activity has always been considered synonymous with synapses, neurotransmitters, and brain cells. So, how does this work? Can brain activity be released from the brain's anatomical structure and function independently? To put it in words that are more relatable, the study focused on how LSD influences dynamics in brain activity, and it investigated the aspect of functional connectivity in the brain, something that most of us have probably never really considered or measured in this way. This specific study, published in the medical journal *NeuroImage,* indicated that, when LSD is administered, a gap starts forming between the brain's anatomical structure and its functional connectivity. Along with this amazing new observation, evidence was also presented that the influence of LSD can increase the intricacy of disconnected brain states. Let's unpack this revelation to truly understand how amazing this is (Dolan, 2021).

The study author, Andrea I. Luppi, notes that the focus of this study was to try and understand the neuroscientific aspect of what it is to be conscious. Luppi is a Gates Scholar in the *Cognition and Consciousness Imaging Group* at Cambridge University. This study appears to be an attempt to unify neurology and metaphysics in a way, and by looking at their conclusion, they might just have succeeded in their quest. The majority of studies conducted on the subject of consciousness have been done with the subject either in a sleeping state, in a state of coma, or under anesthesia. Therefore, researchers wanted to look at another way of understanding consciousness by looking at the altered state of consciousness of a mind that is under the influence of LSD.

It is hard enough to fully understand consciousness itself, but from a scientific perspective, it can be described as the integration of multiplex segregated networks in the brain, as well as their subnetworks. Researchers wanted to understand how the patterns of these segregated networks and subnetworks change over time when the mind is under the influence of LSD. The research team's modus operandi was to work with 15 healthy volunteers during two sessions. They used functional magnetic resonance imaging *(fMRI)* to examine each participant's functional and structural brain activity during both sessions; however, there was only one difference. In the first session, the participants were given a placebo, and in the second session, they were given a dose of LSD.

Activity in the brain is often described as "neurons that fire together, wire together." This is also known as the Hebbian learning rule which states that, if interconnected neurons become active closely in time during a specific event the brain is experiencing, the connection between them becomes stronger, and they eventually create a memory of this event. This means that neurons and neural connections have a type of plasticity as they can be modified or changed based on the fact that their simultaneous activation led to the creation of memory or habit (Krupic, 2017). Now, keeping this in mind, imagine that the brain is now influenced by LSD. When researchers examined the brain activity of participants after ingesting an active dose of LSD, they observed a 'decoupling' between functional and structural connectivity which made brain activity "less constrained than usual by the presence or absence of an underlying anatomical connection" (Dolan, 2021).

In our everyday life, the structure of our brains has a lot of influence over how the brain functions. After these observations, researchers noted that this relationship weakens when LSD is in the system, and that *function* is not as dependent on *structure* as it would be in normal circumstances. Interestingly enough, Luppi noted that this behavior, or change, in the brain is the exact opposite of what happens when there is an influence of anesthesia. So, if the brain's function can be freed from its anatomical structure, what is the brain capable of?

According to the researchers' observations, the brain is then opened to exploring a range of other functional and connectivity patterns that are not prescribed or controlled by the human anatomy. Some of the brain's main functions include integrating and segregating information. LSD has different effects on both functions which fluctuated during the time the substance was in the participants' systems. A common example of "losing yourself" during an LSD trip would be attributed to a high level of integrative activity. However, although these amazing observations have now been captured on LSD and brain function, researchers that participated in the study acknowledge that larger studies need to be done to fully understand this area of neuroscience.

Researchers all agree that this study, and other neuroscientific studies on psychedelics, are invaluable as they provide insight into the brain's chemistry levels and the nature of subjective experiences and brain function. What makes the observations from this study so special is that the brain cannot be described as static in any way, and neither can the conceptual mind (Dolan, 2021). This research expedition provides a glimpse into what happens in your brain physically and chemically when you have a euphoric experience linked to LSD, and the sheer potential our minds are hiding is explained in a more concrete manner.

LSD and MDMA: A New Super Combination?

From a recreational perspective, the combination of LSD and MDMA is known as 'candyflipping.' We're going to discuss the use of this combination that is very far removed from candyflipping; on the contrary, it is the therapeutic possibilities of combining MDMA with LSD. The Psychedelic Pharmaceutical company MindMed is ready to conduct a new Phase 1 Clinical Trial that will focus subjectively on the combination of MDMA and LSD. The main goal of this study is to establish whether MDMA, a substance that is known for generating feelings of wellbeing, can be used as a tool to reduce an unwanted acute sense of negativity that is an effect often seen when administering LSD to patients. In other words, can MDMA be used to reduce this negative symptom of LSD to produce an overall successful outcome in psychedelic-assisted therapy? Researchers are optimistic about the synergistic potential of the two drugs.

Another pro when combining the LSD with MDMA is that the patient will ultimately experience longer-lasting effects. The Phase 1 trial is planned to involve 24 participants, all in a healthy state. The study will follow a four-stage cross-over design, which means that each patient-participant will be blindly undertaking four developmental stages. The four sessions will consist of: 1 MDMA placebo plus 100 micrograms of LSD; next, one LSD placebo and 100mg of MDMA; then, 100mg of MDMA and 100 micrograms of LSD; and finally, an MDMA placebo and an LSD placebo. Researchers aim with the primary outcome to look at the acute subjective influence of each combination. Subjects will also be monitored in terms of heart rate, body temperature, and blood pressure (Haridy, 2020).

This scientific approach to combining MDMA and LSD is being put into practice and tested for the first time even though recreational drug users have been applying this idea for years, hence the term candyflipping. One of the reasons to put this theory into practice is based on the few papers there are that are published on the harmonious effect between MDMA and LSD, and the MindMed trial is expected to take at least twelve months; however, the results may take up to two years before being published (Haridy, 2020). These progressions indicate that scientists, and their research in psychedelics, are taking huge leaps in the right direction. If these different substances are now so well-studied that combinations can be considered, it means that considerable progress has been made.

MindMed is located in Basel, Switzerland, and has also revealed that they are researching what is called an "LSD-neutralizing compound," which can be used to counteract an LSD trip. This can be extremely useful, especially if someone is experiencing a bad trip. If this research is successful, this compound can be used as an "off-switch," and prevent mental damage by neutralizing the effects of LSD.

These further studies of functional-LSD use are groundbreaking and mind-boggling, to say the least; however, from a traditional pharmaceutical perspective, they don't seem to be at the forefront of the development of medical and pharmacological science. There still seems to be that gap between Big Pharma and the independent institutions like MindMed who are conducting these important research studies that specifically focus on psychedelics.

Big Pharma and the Banning of LSD

Big Pharma has a massive customer base when it comes to psychiatric drugs. Additionally, most of these drugs are designed to be taken on a chronic basis, which ensures the pharmaceutical companies a long-lasting income. Referring back to the effects of MDMA treatment for depression in the first chapter, one of the most profound results was how quickly patients' suffering from symptoms of depression started to improve—and this only in one of the primary clinical trials. After all, it's not like these psychiatric disorders are going to disappear. The problem is that psychedelic drugs have the potential to provide longer-lasting effects; however, even though tests indicating these effects have only commenced in recent years, these signs of therapeutic potential were already there in the early studies of these substances. Psychedelic substances and their current treatment results suggest the possibility of either not requiring follow-up treatments or at the very least, follow-up treatments that would be well spaced out as early indications are that positive results from initial treatments last in excess of 6 months or longer.

The pharmaceutical business is a multi-billion dollar industry, and if there is one thing that could ruin this industry, it would be the rise of investor interest in the development of more effective drugs (Eskin, 2021).

- On October 24th, 1968, by Public Law 90-639, the United States made LSD illegal and increased penalties regarding the unlawful act of possessing or consuming LSD.

- Mexico passed a law in 2009 that legalized the possession of 15 micrograms of LSD even though they regulate the substance.

- LSD was decriminalized in Portugal in 2001. Possession of less than 500 µg LSD is not seen as a criminal offense. However the substance can still be seized by law enforcement, and the possessor can be referred to compulsory treatment (Reality Sandwich, 2019a).

The Counterculture Catalyst

Along with the banning of LSD came the persecution of the hippies and the counterculture movement. This appeared to have been an effort by the press and, possibly, the government. In 1966, the LA Times published an article titled *U.S. Plans Intensive Campaign Against LSD*. In this article, the reporter, Rudy Abramson, quotes the FDA as saying that LSD is "almost as dangerous as narcotics" (DiPaolo, 2018). Abramson further wrote that, according to the FDA, LSD is far too accessible to young people and the general public, especially on college campuses. During the same year, the *New Jersey Narcotic Drug Study Commission* gave

LSD another blow by calling the substance the "greatest threat facing the community," and they even went as far as calling LSD "more dangerous than the Vietnam War." It didn't end there, though. To further wage war against LSD, *Science Magazine* published an article in 1967 that claimed that LSD could damage human chromosomes. Because these sources were all deemed trustworthy by society, the information was ingested without question. A clinical study conducted in 1971 and published in the National Library of Medicine, indicated that LSD, even with regular recreational use, does not have the potential to damage chromosomes. This refuted the claims in *Science Magazine*'s 1976 article (Dishotsky et al., 1971).

Some academics also say that the banning of LSD was motivated by an orchestrated effort of exaggeration, stereotyping, sensationalization, and the distortion of facts. This approach raised a sense of moral panic among members of society and a hostile attitude towards the hippies and their use of LSD. They were seen as the enemies; the ones promoting unconventional living, sexual liberation, and moving away from societal structures; they were synonymous with the widespread stigma of LSD. The banning of LSD most likely received the most media attention out of all of the psychedelic drugs, and therefore, because it is such a well-known talking point among academics and other fervent investigators, there are several interesting theories as to why this substance was taken down and crucified.

LSD Today

The reason why there is a growing interest in LSD research again dates back to studies conducted four decades ago, and the focus of the research is to treat anxiety disorders linked to patients with terminal illnesses, depression, PTSD, and drug addiction. It seems quite counter-intuitive to try and treat drug addiction with what is also considered to be a recreational drug; however, the methods of administration and dosages differ largely between a recreational approach and a therapeutic approach. The way LSD works in order to achieve these results is described by researchers in an eerily similar manner to how Timothy Leary described why he needed psilocybin for his Ego Obliteration ritual: the use of LSD creates an impression of weakening the ego or bringing it down to earth, which helps individuals to put their issues in perspective by being able to see their life in a bigger picture.

As with magic mushrooms, microdosing is also popular when it comes to LSD; but because of the fact that this substance is so much more potent than psilocybin, one needs to be very careful when it comes to establishing and measuring the dosage. Interestingly enough, microdosing with LSD has become very popular among individuals whose work requires creative thinking, like marketing executives, artists, and musicians. An article on microdosing also reports that drug dealers that deal in psychedelic drugs have noticed an increase in microdosing requests; that is, to buy the substance already measured into the required micro dosage. Creatives laud this method of taking LSD for enhancing their ability to do their jobs and finishing projects they have previously been struggling with. Others claim that, instead of feeling like they want to escape their lives, microdosing makes them want to embrace their lives because of how it makes them feel open and accepting of their life situation (Kitchens, 2018).

The Israeli-American author, Ayelet Waldman, who is famous for her book *A Really Good Day*, is considered a notable influencer for LSD microdosing. In her book, she documented her personal experiences while microdosing with LSD for a month, and she had only praise for this method of treating mental disorders and depression, even though it is still mostly considered highly unorthodox. Her book is a testimony of how LSD microdosing helped her to overcome the debilitating symptoms of mood disorders and anxiety. In her book, she includes the opinion of one of her daughters, who comments that she has been able to control her emotions much more efficiently, especially when she is angry. Waldman used a guide authored by a United States psychologist, James Fadiman, Ph.D., to structure her microdosing, and this forms part of her book's content. Fadiman's book is called *The Psychedelic Explorer's Guide: Safe, Therapeutic, and Sacred Journeys,* published in 2011, and is basically the Microdosing Bible. In it, you will find all the ground rules for microdosing safely and responsibly for whatever reason you may need to do so (Mammoser, 2017).

LSD may be the most controversial psychedelic of them all—and for good reason. Abused by the CIA, demonized by what appears to be an organized press campaign, and banned by the U.S. government, it took dedication from those who believed in, and still do believe in, the healing potential of psychedelic substances. And, as the most recent and upcoming trials suggest, these beliefs have not been in vain.

Becoming an Underground LSD Guide

You'd be surprised at how many people have lost their trust in pharmaceutical medicine and have turned to other alternative treatments—many of them to psychedelics. And in this context, we are not referring to Timothy Leary-style, hedonistic, recreational psychedelic use, but rather the use of substances like LSD in a therapeutic setting. Of course, if you are not a participant in an official research trial, you have to find another way to get this treatment. Additionally, you don't only need the substance itself, but you need someone who can serve as a guide while you are under the influence.

Here's where many people have started a side-hustle—so hush-hush that not even their spouses, best friends, or any of their family members know about it. Introducing the underground LSD guide—a person who gets paid to look after someone who wants to self-medicate with substances, such as LSD, while in the comfort of their own home, but needs a guardian to guide them through their trips. A psychedelic guide might meet up with a client in a home or a rented space, dose them, and sit with them, waiting while they trip it out. Unlike a psychotherapist with an educational background, an underground guide does not have any educational requirements. They are uneducated guardians who look after the welfare of those who need treatment for their mental health, and many of them see it as their calling as, while they experience their 'patient' going through their trippy motions, they can also sometimes see the demons they are struggling with (Dunne, 2018).

Dosage Guide

The safest way to get an accurate dose of LSD is by using an instrument that can measure micrograms. A standard dose for inducing psychedelic experiences can range from 50 to 150 micrograms. For microdosing, the majority of users consume about a tenth of the normal recreational dose, so this means that a microdose is somewhere between five to fifteen micrograms.

Recreational Dose	150 μg (enough to get you trippin')	270 μg (normal)	300 μg (strong)
Microdose	5 μg (small dose)	10 μg (normal)	15 μg (high)

Chapter 4:
The Truth About DMT

Ever heard of DMT? It's not quite as famous as our previous psychedelic friends, but those who use it know that if you want your trip to be potent, DMT is the way to go. It packs a punch. This fascinating psychedelic has also been studied for quite a while and has a rich history of use in religious and spiritual rituals. It's quite an amazing substance, actually. Let's take a look.

What is DMT?

DMT is an abbreviation for Dimethyltryptamine, a hallucinogenic tryptamine that is a natural but very powerful psychedelic compound. It is related to LSD which, as we know by now, is also a powerful psychedelic substance. Though it is not as famous or notorious as LSD or psilocybin, it is known for causing brief and unforgettably vivid trips. Therefore, it is referred to as the "spirit molecule."

DMT also has its own street names. You might hear it referred to as one of the following:

- Dimitri
- A businessman's trip
- A businessman's special
- Fantasia
- Forty-five-minute psychosis

An interesting fact about this substance is that it has no effect when taken orally (unless an MAOI is added) because the digestive system destroys the psychedelic components which would normally cause the trip. Thus, it has to be injected, smoked, or sniffed for the user to get the desired trippy effects. DMT takes the user on a short, wild ride that lasts about an hour and starts approximately five minutes after the substance is injected, smoked, or sniffed. Research has shown that a form of DMT produced naturally by the human body is present in the bodily fluids of people that suffer from Schizophrenia, and although there is not an abundance of evidence, there are strong speculations that DMT is produced naturally in the pineal gland, a small pea-sized and mysterious component of the brain.

Due to the fact that DMT is a naturally occurring tryptamine, derivatives of it can be found in at least 400 species of fungi and other plants. DMT can also be referred to as a core tryptamine because basically all substances belonging to the tryptamine class contain the chemical structure of DMT—psilocybin being the most prevalent. Chemists can produce DMT via both extraction or synthesis, although, due to costs, extraction has become much more popular than synthetic production. DMT usually takes the shape of a pale yellow or a white crystal in powdered form.

Some of the most well-known forms of DMT include:

- Acetate
- Freebase
- Hydrochloride
- Citrate
- Fumarate

All of the above forms are crystallized compounds containing different bases or acids that are used to bind the molecules. Acetate, citrate, and hydrochloride are all examples of DMT salts where a different acid is used to produce the salt. These different forms also require different methods of consumption. Users typically consume DMT by vaporizing it to a temperature of 160 degrees Celsius (320°F), but it can also be consumed orally by combining it with an MAOI or intranasally.

Vaporized DMT has to be in its freebase form because theories state that the salts release toxic components once heated. A common misconception about vaporized DMT is that someone can consume it successfully when smoking it using a direct open flame. This, however, is not accurate; applying a direct open flame to a freebase form of DMT will cause it to burn and subsequently become inactive. DMT instead becomes activated when it is vaporized at a temperature around 160 degrees Celsius (320°F). You can prolong the effects of vaporized DMT by mixing it with changa, a smoking blend, which typically contains plants or other components that contain the necessary MAOI, or to which an MAOI component was added.

Those who partake may also choose to snort DMT, which is a lot easier if it's in its salt forms, such as citrate, fumarate, or acetate. Snorting causes better absorption through the mucous membranes.

Finally, DMT can be consumed orally, but it needs to be combined with an MAOI. This method of consumption is utilized in different ways. For example, one method involves cooking different plants containing these compounds for a few hours. Some users have learned to simplify this method by first extracting the active compounds, and then consuming them in a pill form, which is commonly known as "pillahuasca," or the "parachute" form. "Parachute" form is when a user places the active substances inside a thin paper, such as tissue paper, then swallows it. When someone decides to use a pharmaceutical type MAOI, the end result is referred to as "pharmahuasca."

There are indigenous groups from the Amazon region who consume a combination of DMT and an MAOI by combining two specific plants known as the *Banisteriopsis caapi,* which is also called ayahuasca, or just "caapi," and the plant *Psychotria viridis,* or *alba,* which is also known as "chacruna." These plants are cooked together in a large pot while these indigenous groups perform a spiritual ritual. The next chapter will focus on ayahuasca, its history, and its use in detail (Reality Sandwich, 2019a).

DMT's chemical root structure is very close to a medication called *sumatriptan,* used to treat migraines. This is because both of these substances act as a non-selective agonist to serotonin receptors, especially the 5-HT2A receptor. We've been introduced to serotonin before in previous chapters, and looking back, we can now conclude with confidence that serotonin is a very important neurotransmitter in the brain that affects and regulates many of our behaviors. It is safe to say that most psychedelics have this common function; they like playing with the serotonin receptors in the brain. DMT, like psilocybin, has a history that dates far back. Historians don't fight about the history of

DMT as much as they do with magic mushrooms, and it might be due to the discovery of DMT's existence in a place they least expected.

History and Traditional Use

As has been discovered, DMT is not only naturally present in our bodies but also in nature, and specifically in certain plants. It is estimated to have been used in rituals for centuries in South America. Some even speculate that the indigenous peoples from this continent started using DMT as far back as four millennia. What we know for sure is that, although ancient indigenous peoples likely didn't have a name for DMT, nor were they able to identify the specific compound in the plants, they were nonetheless able to identify which specific plants could produce the mystical psychedelic brew called ayahuasca, thus producing the effects necessary for their spiritual and religious ceremonies. It is here where we should mention that DMT and ayahuasca have a lot in common. The ayahuasca brew is traditionally consumed orally and as we now know, DMT requires an MAOI to activate it in the digestive system. The ancient indigenous tribes knew something of this when they combined two plants to make their ayahuasca brew, which could be explained as producing an extended DMT trip. It is only recently that science has caught up and been able to identify the two components that create this otherworldly experience.

The natural form of DMT can also be found in a hallucinogenic snuff called *cohoba*. This snuff is made from the seeds of the *Piptadenia peregrina*, a tree native to South America. This snuff is known to have been used by the Llanos and the Indians of Trinidad in the Northern parts of South America during the earlier Spanish visits to the continent. Of course, DMT can also be synthesized in a laboratory (The Editors of Encyclopaedia Britannica, 2018; Davis, 2017).

DMT was first synthesized in a laboratory in the 1930s, but the first studies were conducted in the 1950s by the Hungarian psychologist and chemist, Stephen Szára, who used volunteers to conduct his studies. Funnily enough, Szára was originally interested in LSD, but after the Big Pharma company, Sandoz, rejected his work on the grounds of LSD being a dangerous substance, he turned his attention to DMT. He later started working for the United States National Institutes of Health (Strassman, 2001).

DMT mainly affects the user psychologically by causing euphoria, visual and auditory hallucinations, and an altered sense of space and time. There are many accounts of users' life-altering experiences where they talked to creatures resembling elves. Elves seen in these trips are so common that they've been dubbed "DMT elves" or "machine elves," and they are usually perceived to be visiting from other worlds. These users talk about complete shifts in their perception of their own reality and identity. When DMT is smoked, specifically, users describe their experiences as otherworldly, being in an alternate reality, or even having a near-death experience. An interesting perspective regarding these intense experiences is that users that have also experimented with other substances, such as psilocybin and LSD, say that DMT has a far more potent trip experience; however, it has the least side effects from any of the substances they've used.

Studies and Interesting Findings

Stephen Szára Taking the First Step

Stephen Szára, whom we mentioned earlier, is the chemist we now know started the research journey on DMT. When Szára started working in the United States, he started working with Julius Axelrod, among others, to investigate the metabolism of DMT and other related substances and compounds on volunteers that suffer from Schizophrenia. While conducting their research, the team made a breakthrough by being able to characterize three co-generative hallucinogenic substances of tryptamine, namely diethyl-tryptamine, dimethyl-tryptamine, and dipropyl-tryptamine, also known abbreviated as DET, DMT, and DPT. Through this identification and classification, they were able to describe the effects and pharmacokinetics of each co-generative substance.

Szára's research remained focused on DMT in particular, and he hypothesized that DMT, specifically, had the potential to cause hallucinogenic experiences and be a contributing factor to psychosis in the brain. Szára strongly felt that any hallucinogenic drugs should be approached and studied in a questioning manner, hoping that this heuristic approach may help researchers understand the mechanisms of these substances and how they affect the brain, to then further understand the brain-mind relationship better (Szára, 1994).

Rick Strassman and the Spirit Molecule

Rick Strassman, a clinical associate professor in the field of psychiatry for the University of New Mexico's School of Medicine, is famous for his book *DMT: The Spirit Molecule,* which is a summary of his experiments with DMT on humans, other experimental studies, and his own reflections and opinions about what he has discovered through these studies and trials. Strassman, fueled by his interest in the nature of human consciousness, started his research on the hormone melatonin and the pineal gland in the brain, which is also said to secrete DMT. This was during the 1980s, and at the time, there was evidence suggesting that melatonin had psychoactive effects. The hormone melatonin influences sleep in human beings and it is light-sensitive; after conducting several experiments using bright lights, he came to the conclusion that melatonin only had sedative properties, which caused his focus to shift to DMT (Strassman et al., 1987).

Strassmann led a government-approved and government-funded clinical research project in the first half of the '90s at the University of New Mexico. DMT was the focal point of this study, and he tested it on human subjects in various speculative conditions. His former work with melatonin directly inspired this study. Strassman wanted to identify the effects of DMT on brain activity, as the substance is closely related to melatonin, as well as the neurotransmitter serotonin. It was from his findings in this study that Strassman coined the term "spirit molecule," which also inspired his famous book. During his studies on human subjects, he observed many recurring incidents that included elements of religious experiences. These experiences manifested in hearing voices, seeing visions, a sense of disembodied consciousness, unusual insights, dynamic and forceful emotions, and the appearance of the subject feeling overwhelmingly significant or special. We can substantiate these recurring observations because, during the five-year study, the research team, with Strassman included, administered as many as 400 doses of DMT to almost 60 human volunteers (Roberts, 2014).

Strassman subsequently attributed both the psychological effects and biological effects he observed in his studies as effects that DMT has on central and peripheral serotonin receptors by activating them. Along with this influential study came another scientific article describing a new scale that can be used to measure psychological effects of psychedelic substances, called the HRS, or the Hallucinogen Rating Scale (Strassman, 1994).

Due to his research subjects experiencing contact with transcendental beings, and having transcendental experiences, Strassman hypothesized that when a human has a near-death experience or is close to dying, the pineal gland may secrete an increased supply of DMT, making them see visions and transcendental beings before the moment of death. A follow-up study also proved that DMT is unique to other hallucinogenic substances, as the administration of doses that are too closely spaced showed a lack of tolerance for the effects of DMT. This refers to the potency of the substance and, due to this fact, dosages should be spaced farther apart than, for example, administering two doses of psilocybin to a patient in one therapy session.

Before Rick Strassman discovered everything that he did about DMT while conducting his study and writing his book, he appeared to be a man searching for meaning in his own, younger life. He started taking LSD in the early '70s, and it led him to start a religious journey with Eastern Buddhism. After training in Zen Buddhism for 20 years, he became part of a Western Buddhism order, and he himself led the meditation group within this order. Then, he made a bizarre decision. After being so devoted to Buddhism for 20 years, he underwent a curious change of heart when he discovered DMT, and his work with this substance led him to the conclusion that the Buddhist principles practice cannot explain the spiritual experience provided by DMT. To him, DMT had no feasible explanation. Instead, he came to the conclusion that DMT experiences may be more closely related to prophecies from the Hebrew Bible. You would expect his motivation for this to be more on the irrational side, but it is clear that sober deliberation inspired this conclusion:

> *"I worked through various models' methods of understanding the DMT volunteers' experiences and found them wanting. The Buddhist psychological model didn't comport with the data—the "more real than real" element of volunteers' experiences (Buddhism proposes these phenomena are all generated by the mind, rather than "real" observations of external reality); [this] did nothing to suggest a satisfactory evolutionary explanation for the presence of DMT in the human body"* (Solomon, 2011).

Strassman further commented that, when subjects take DMT, their experience is different from other psychedelic drugs, as they are able to maintain their sense of self while having visions and other hallucinatory experiences. When taking, for example, LSD, one gets the feeling of losing oneself as part of the experience, which also happens with other psychedelic drugs, and this sets DMT apart from these substances.

DMT for Major Depression

The study of DMT for major depression can definitely be called a breakthrough. The *UK Medicines and Healthcare products Regulatory Agency*, or the MHRA, has granted approval for clinical testing of DMT in 2020 to measure its efficacy specifically in the case of major depressive disorder or MDD. This is a Phase I trial, which means that the research study is still conducted on a small scale, and testing will be done on only a few, healthy patients. Major depressive disorder affects the lives of approximately 16 million people in the United States alone.

This trial will be conducted by the neuro-pharmaceutical company, SmallPharma, which will be collaborating with the Imperial College of London's Centre for Psychedelic Research. The structure of the trial is carefully planned, and it will start by combining DMT with psychotherapy and counseling. As we've discussed different psychedelic substances throughout the book, we've come to know that this is now an age-old method that has been used in therapeutic methods, as with MDMA, magic mushrooms, and LSD to some extent. A refined development of this method can specifically be linked to extensive research conducted at Johns Hopkins University. Researchers describe taking a dose of DMT before undergoing therapy as the same process should you take a snowglobe and shake it vigorously to get all the 'snowflakes' up in the air and allow them to settle spontaneously. This translates into the psychedelic drug breaking up all the contemplative thought processes in your head and undoing subsequent developing conditions like depressive thoughts, ideas, and feelings of stress. This opens up the brain to form new and healthy connections, which can be re-enforced during a therapy session.

Carol Routledge, the chief medical and scientific officer at Small Pharma described the upcoming research studies as a ground-breaking moment in medical science's quest to treat major depression effectively and safely, as current circumstances brought on in 2020 cause more and more people to suffer from this condition. Routledge also explained that the company chose to focus on DMT, omitting psilocybin as an option, as they think DMT has specific medical advantages that are distinct from other psychedelic drugs. The brevity of a DMT trip in comparison with those induced by psilocybin, for example, and the level of intensity compared in the same way, shows that DMT has superior therapeutic advantages and benefits. She further emphasized that the patients will be tested using pure DMT that is not mixed with other substances. Although this is the Phase 1 trial, the company hopes to make a difference in the treatment of major depression and provide treatment that has fewer side effects, longer-lasting effects of relief, and is more accessible to the public (MacKenzie, 2020; Geddes, 2020).

DMT for Substance Abuse Disorders

Considering all of the psychedelic substances we've covered, some of them include promising research for the treatment of substance abuse disorders and addictive behavior, it feels like a mental leap to try and understand how DMT can be used in these cases, specifically because it is in some cases very different from other hallucinogens. That's what makes a preliminary study about DMT and substance abuse disorders so intriguing. For substance abuse disorders, the company Entheon Biomedical wants to look at the possibility of therapeutically using DMT by administering it intravenously. Two of the company's biggest concerns are the efficacy and the safety of this method.

Entheon Biomedical made a clinical study agreement with the organization, the *Centre for Human Drug Research* (CHDR), that is located in Leiden in the Netherlands. This agreement is to conduct early-phase clinical trials on humans using DMT. Researchers specifically want to look at contributing factors like pharmacokinetics and the pharmacodynamics of DMT. Although the aim of the research is to test DMT's ability as a therapeutic or treatment aid for substance abuse disorders, researchers want to take small steps by first looking at how the substance reacts physiologically and biochemically, especially since it's being administered intravenously.

This first trial will also provide researchers with further knowledge on how DMT will affect an individual's central nervous system and the participants' subjective experiences. These different types of information are crucial for determining whether there is potential for further study, specifically for the treatment of substance abuse disorders. Extensive studies of the previous academic and scientific literature have also been conducted to establish the preliminary potential of DMT for this specific use. Some of the reasons why it gets the green checkmark are because of its high therapeutic potential and it is considered to have a 'safer' status regarding its toxicology profile—probably because it also exists endogenously; additionally, because the body metabolizes DMT quickly and effectively, it shows potential for a shorter type of therapeutic experience that can lead to cost-efficiency, and make therapy sessions and strategies more flexible. F

The study is looking at specific conditions in their preliminary study. These conditions include alcohol addiction, nicotine dependency, and the disordered use of opioids. The protocol of the research study is to identify and look for ways to address the underlying factors that cause addictive behavior. The theory that supports the DMT-assisted protocol is that this behavior comes from a complex emotional and psychological place in the mind and that DMT has the potential to target this 'space' directly where it is hypothesized all substance abuse and addictive behavior stem from. So, the study wants to hit this target first, see if the administering of DMT is as effective as they think it will be, and then expand on their research to also cover other indications and a more diverse collection of substance abuse or addictive disorders.

The goal projection is to be in the final stages of the study within the next 4 to 5 years, so it appears that scientists are highly confident about the success of this research study. There is a dire need for a feasible treatment that can help individuals cope with substance abuse and addictive behavior, especially during the COVID-19 pandemic, and the company recognizes this urgent need for new medical and therapeutic solutions (MacKenzie, 2021).

Yes, the Spirit Molecule is Also Being Tested as a Remedy for Stroke

This one is quite amazing. Up to this point, research into psychedelics has mainly focused on treatment for mental health, but it appears that this line has now been transcended and plans are being made to test the elements of this substance on the debilitating effects of stroke. Algernon Pharmaceuticals has already laid out a full research study protocol for the treatment of stroke and is ready to start conducting ground-breaking experiments using this unique psychedelic substance.

Algernon is a clinical-stage pharmaceutical development company, and they announced on February 21st, 2021 that they are going forward with a clinical study, using DMT to research new treatment methods for stroke. Algernon will be the first company in the world to pursue the treatment of stroke using a psychedelic substance and, although a commencement date has not been set, the company wants to start its clinical research trials as soon as possible.

As part of their preparation, Algernon has filed new patents for new types of DMT in the provisional form, as well as for methods of use, dosage, and formulation regarding ischemic stroke. Additionally, the company wants to combine DMT treatment with *Constraint-Induced Movement Therapy,* or CIMT. CIMT is a rehabilitation approach used for individuals who have suffered a stroke where the patient is forced to use the affected limb. This is achieved by restraining the functional or less-affected limb like the patient's other arm and letting the patient conduct a series of exercises for several hours (Corbetta et al., 2016). It appears that the pharmacological process is going to be to repurpose DMT by not using its psychedelic components in the treatment for stroke.

Algernon's decision to move on to conducting human trials is supported by several independent preclinical studies that all showed positive results. These studies, which were conducted on mice, indicated for example, that DMT assisted with restoring neural plasticity on functional and structural levels, and that DMT also helped the promotion of neurogenesis, which is the development and growth of tissue in the brain. An example of a recent study that indicates promising results, showed that DMT helped rats recover more quickly by speeding up the recovery of motor function, and these rats showed lower levels of lesions in the control group of animals that did not receive DMT treatment. As losing motor function in the face and limbs are some of the most debilitating after-effects of a stroke, these results appear promising and set the stage for further clinical research.

During their trials, Algernon wants to focus on a continuous flow of the intravenous administration of DMT, and therefore they want the level of the dose to be a microdose or a sub-hallucinogenic dose. The company is also using the microdosing approach for another reason. They believe that using the substance in such small quantities makes their findings and data more acceptable and subsequently reviewable with the aim to achieve clinical acceptance. Their strategy may give them easier access to regulatory approval along with a Breakthrough Therapy designation they require from the FDA.

Algernon is deviating from the main studies involving DMT by specifically focusing on its non-psychedelic components and its healing and therapeutic qualities. This is a first when it comes to psychedelic research, as the focus has always been on the psychedelic component itself and its partner in crime, the mental aspect (Algernon Pharmaceuticals, 2021).

Big Pharma and the Banning of DMT

The reason why psychedelic drugs are declared illegal always has an interesting backstory. The main reason why DMT was declared illegal is because of a blanket ban on all psychotropic substances by the United Nations that was inspired by the United States' banning of LSD in 1968. After the banning of LSD in 1968, the United Nations held a *United Nations Convention on Psychotropic Drugs* in 1971, and the subsequent agreement was signed by all countries across the globe except Haiti, Liberia, the Solomon Islands, Vanuatu, Samoa, Liberia, Kiribati, East Timor, Tuvalu, and Equatorial Guinea.

This inevitably caused DMT to become a Schedule 1 drug just like LSD, psilocybin, and MDMA in the United States. However, the state of Oregon, which seems to be the forerunner on decriminalizing psychedelic substances, decriminalized DMT in 2020, along with all other illegal substances and drugs.

DMT is prohibited in most countries. There are, however, some exceptions; the ayahuasca brew, which contains DMT and is often used for spiritual and religious purposes, is exempt in some Central and South American countries. Ayahuasca is currently legal to use and possess in Brazil. Similarly, Peru is known for ayahuasca, so use and possession are permitted. In Colombia, there are no specific laws related to DMT use, possibly because ayahuasca is considered a religious sacrament. The same goes for Uruguay, Ecuador, and Costa Rica. In most cases, DMT is still a controlled substance. As an aside, due to the permitted use of DMT/ayahuasca in the above-mentioned countries for the purposes of spiritual or religious ceremonies, ayahuasca tourism has become popular.

No laws prohibiting ayahuasca in Italy currently exist, but there have been recent conflicts with law enforcement due to the use of ayahuasca in the Santo Daime Church, a congregation of forest-based religious followers. Similar to Italy, there are no specific laws that prohibit ayahuasca in Spain. Still, the same conflicts with law enforcement happen to members of the Santo Daime Church for using ayahuasca in their religious ceremonies. Germany does not have specific ayahuasca laws, but DMT is illegal under the German Narcotics Act. Any and all DMT-containing plants are also illegal to cultivate, transport, and possess in France.

Australia has harsh laws for various drugs, including DMT. However, there have been no prosecutions up to date.

In the Netherlands, DMT is listed as a Schedule I prohibited substance under their Opium Law. Here, ayahuasca became illegal on October 1st, 2019. The reason for this ruling is based on an incident where a woman tried to import 33 kgs worth of ayahuasca brew across the border. After the lower court found her guilty, she appealed the issue to the Supreme Court on the account that the guilty finding would be a repression of her religious freedom. The Supreme Court, however, focused on public health and ruled that her importation of such a large quantity of ayahuasca was an infringement on public health, which made it an illegal act. It is, however, still unlikely that an individual will be prosecuted for personal possession of ayahuasca in the Netherlands. (Reality Sandwich, 2019a).

The mainstream view of DMT remains very misinformed, possibly due to Big Pharma and the government, which is that when one takes DMT, hallucinations lead one away from reality and can cause one to go 'crazy.' However, there is another side to DMT, not only for those who use it for religious and spiritual experiences—it also has possible therapeutic potential.

In the end, the reason why DMT is banned by the government is the same reason why all psychedelics are banned or classified as Schedule I. The government would rather allow the public to use mind-altering, mind-restricting substances, like alcohol, and keep them away from mind-opening substances, like psychedelics. Further, it is the view of some that Big Pharma objects to the legalization of products or substances for which there is little in the way of profit for them, or for the chance at gaining repeat customers. Of course, these opinions are open for debate.

DMT Today

Since microdosing became popular, DMT was, of course, included in the substances considered relevant. Clinical doses of DMT that were used in trials were mostly measured by looking at the weight of the participant. For example, a clinical dose of DMT would range from 0.05 mg per kg to 1 mg per kg of a participant. The clinical purpose of DMT was not to put a participant on a massive trip, so this can be considered a reasonably small dose, especially at the smaller end of the scale. To put it in perspective, if a participant weighed 150lbs (70kg), a clinical dose can vary from 35mg to 70mg of DMT. There is a large difference there, but one also needs to consider that DMT was used in research for different types of conditions, and not all of them were psychological.

A microdose is not supposed to include any of the acute effects that one would commonly experience when taking a recreational dose of DMT. In contrast, taking it on a regular basis should provide lasting psychological and socially linked benefits to the individual microdosing. One of the common ways of knowing you've consumed a dosage that is above the requirements of a microdose, is experiencing typical DMT-related effects like the "sound of silence." The required effects of a microdose include an increased sense of mindfulness, decreased levels of anxiety and depression, improved concentration, and an overall improvement in one's well being. In order for DMT microdosing to be as effective as possible, each dose consumed needs to be accurately measured.

Some of DMT's most common effects include dilated pupils, feeling dizzy, feeling agitated, bizarre rapid and rhythmic eye movements, increased heart rate and blood pressure, and a feeling of tightness in the chest or chest pain. If you decide to take your DMT orally, you may also vomit, have diarrhea, or feel nauseous. What can make DMT dangerous is, not every user will require the same dosage of the substance, so it's likely that some users need to use less. If you take just a little too much, your trip may be so frightening, and the experience so overwhelming, that you may need professional help to process what you witnessed during your trip.

It is important for an individual who has a history of Schizophrenia or epilepsy to first consult with a medical practitioner before using DMT, even in microdosing forms, and for anyone else who wants to use DMT, it is crucial to know that DMT cannot be taken in conjunction with other psychedelics such as MDMA, mescaline, or any other phenethylamine—the results can be fatal.

Finally, it's good to know that DMT alone has a very low risk of overdose. The most current studies suggest that an individual can ingest even more than 5.5 grams of DMT and still survive. This is, more or less, 30 times the common recreational dose. Although such a high dose may not be fatal, it will most probably provide an extremely unpleasant experience that you'd never want to relive again. The most common reason for fatalities linked with DMT is the mixing of psychedelic substances, or if an individual is using it while also having a pre-existing condition. If the DMT dose is unreasonably high—in this case, higher than the 'high' dose we mentioned—it can cause respiratory arrest and possibly even place the user in a coma.

The reason for banning DMT is no different than for any other psychedelic substance. On the one hand, they pose a threat to Big

Pharma, and on the other hand, the government prefers the public to use drugs developed and manufactured by Big Pharma companies, as there is a wide circle of individuals who benefit from this process financially.

We Need to Talk About DMT and Serotonin Syndrome Disorder

When taking DMT, especially a higher dose, it can cause your brain to release very high levels of serotonin. Now, that can't be bad, right? Unfortunately, the saying "too much of a good thing" also applies to serotonin, and when your brain releases too much of this neurotransmitter, you can find yourself with a life-threatening condition called Serotonin Syndrome Disorder.

People who are most likely to get this disorder are people who take DMT while also taking antidepressants, especially antidepressants that act as MAOIs. If you know that you've taken this class of antidepressant and also DMT, be on the lookout for the following symptoms:

- disorientation
- anxiety
- rigid muscles
- spasmodic muscles
- shivering
- overactive reflexes
- dilated pupils
- tremors

- irritability
- confusion

Seek immediate medical attention as these two components in your body can cause a life-threatening condition. When it comes to other substances and medication, also avoid mixing DMT with the following:

- ketamine
- psilocybin
- benzodiazepines (sleeping pills)
- LSD
- opioids
- cocaine
- cannabis
- gamma-hydroxybutyric acid, or GHB
- any muscle relaxants
- alcohol
- amphetamines

These substances all have an effect on the central nervous system, just like anti-depressants, and can cause adverse effects when combined with DMT, especially if you are not clued up about how powerful DMT is (Santos-Longhurst & Carter, 2019).

To conclude, research conducted on DMT is showing that it has the potential to not only aid in the healing of mental illness but also in other severe and debilitating conditions, meaning that this psychedelic substance is the first that has the potential to be used therapeutically without harnessing its psychedelic components. However, due to its potency, recreational users, and even those who want to self-medicate, need to be extremely careful if they are not using DMT under the supervision of a health practitioner, especially if they are mixing substances.

Dosage Guide

For smoking, the average dose of DMT is approximately 30 to 150mg, and you'll feel the effects almost instantly. You'll experience a peak between the first 3 to 5 minutes, and thereafter a plateau that will last between 45 minutes and an hour. These dosages are all applicable to DMT that is smoked or vaporized (Reality Sandwich, 2019a).

Recreational Dose	2-5 mg (threshold)	10-20 mg (light)	20-40 mg (common)	40-60 ug (strong)

To accurately measure out a DMT microdose, you will need a precision scale that can measure to the precision of 0.001 milligrams—also referred to as a jewelers scale. There is no specific guideline for how much DMT is required for microdosing, but staying under the limit of doses used for research can be a wise guideline. An example of such a DMT dose can range from 0.05 mg/kg to 1 mg/kg, as previously mentioned in a note on clinical trials.

Chapter 5:
All-Natural Ayahuasca

Ayahuasca has a strong connection with DMT, and we know for sure that this psychedelic substance has been used medicinally for thousands of years. This fascinating concoction has the ability to put you on an eight-hour psychedelic journey, and interestingly enough, the ancient use of ayahuasca is not that far removed from the reasons modern individuals use it today. The meaning of the word ayahuasca is still under debate, but experts think that it is closely linked to a phrase like "vine of the spirits." However, due to an immediate after-effect from the consumption of the brew being vomiting, some shamans refer to ayahuasca simply as "la purga."

What is Ayahuasca?

Ayahuasca is essentially a brew made by combining the vine of the plant *Banisteriopsis caapi* with a plant that contains DMT, known as the *Psychotria viridis*. If you brew these two plants together, they have a special way of working in tandem to create special effects in the body. First, the vine of the *B. caapi* contains an MAOI, which works by slowing down the body's ability to metabolize the DMT that is also ingested. This allows the DMT to become active in the body. However, the 'recipe' used for the brew may vary from shaman to shaman, or from person to person. For example, some individuals or shamans use *Peganum harmala*, instead of the MAOI activating ingredient, and the inner root bark of the DMT-containing ingredient, called *acacia confusa* can also be used instead of the leaves, which are normally used.

There are less common ways to create this brew, and it can even be created in the form of snuff. There are shamans who use tobacco-containing plants like *Nicotiana rustica* as a way to smoke the combination; or, they use it as a snuff to calm down participants who will be part of a religious or spiritual ceremony.

The preparation for the brew or snuff is done by grinding up the two main ingredients. Some shamans make their snuff by grinding up the pods of a plant colloquially known as *Yopo*. The traditional way, though, is to combine the two ingredients named at the beginning; the *Banisteriopsis caapi*, which acts as an MAOI, and the DMT-containing plant named *Psychotria viridis*. Because the ways to prepare ayahuasca can vary, this also means that the effects of the substance will vary in terms of its potency and the effects it has on the consumer (Reality Sandwich, 2019).

Ayahuasca Goes by Many Names

This cultural and spiritual beverage is not solely known by the name ayahuasca. There are names linked to different regions, and the brew is known to have as many as dozens of different names across the Amazon, South America, and today, worldwide. The term 'ayahuasca' is derived from a language called Quechua. In Spanish, ayahuasca is called *ayahuasca*; in Portuguese, it is known as *aioasca*; and in Quechua, it is called *ayawasca*.

In Brazil, the brew has quite a few names, including *uni, nixi, caapi, damie, pãe,* and *camarampi*. While *damie* has a set list of ingredients, the other names refer to different combinations of ingredients used to make the brew at the discretion of the shaman making it. In the Putumayo region, which is the South-East region of Columbia, the indigenous people know ayahuasca as a slightly different brew, which they call *yage*. Yage is different as the *Psychotria viridis* is replaced with the leaves of another plant called the *Diplopterys cabrerana,* and this is supposed to make the brew much stronger. The word ayahuasca, as mentioned, is still up for debate, having a complicated and spiritually connotated meaning. It is known that the word 'huasca' or 'wasca' refers to a rope or a vine, and the general interpretation of the word is that it is a vine that leads one to the spiritual world. However, some interpret 'aya' as the spirit or the soul, while others interpret it as death (Reality Sandwich, 2019).

History and Traditional Use

Not much is known about the use of ayahuasca before 2000 B.C., from when the earliest archeological findings date back to. The evidence, however, indicates the regular use of these hallucinogenic or psychedelic plants in the Amazon region in South America. Despite these archeological findings, experts cannot estimate when exactly humans started using ayahuasca, though. Anthropologists and plant experts, like ethnobotanists, are also still at a loss about how these two specific plants, that grow among thousands of different plant species in the Amazon forest, were so expertly identified and combined to create such a potent hallucinogenic brew with these specific prolonged effects. Could it have been by chance?

Another fascinating component of the history of ayahuasca is that evidence exists of its use by multiple tribes throughout the Amazon rainforest and further into South America—indigenous tribes from Ecuador, Colombia, Brazil, Bolivia, and Peru are all known to have used ayahuasca. In each case, it is known by a different name, and there are slight differences to the recipes these varying indigenous peoples are known to use. What's more, each tribe has a different story regarding the origin of their use of ayahuasca. Many believe that the ancient shamans got the recipe from the Amazon "plant teachers," however, archeologists do not find this explanation satisfactory, and they are still looking for the origin of the brew.

Experts have found that the indigenous people of South America have used ayahuasca for many different ailments and ceremonial purposes. What happened at these indigenous ceremonies, especially during ancient times, is unknown to us, and as we know that there were many different tribes using the brew, there must have been different ceremonial traditions and applications of ayahuasca. Over the millennia that these ceremonies have existed, they have changed, evolved, and acclimated among the indigenous peoples who still practice them. Although they are diverse and have changed through their many years of existence, there are some traditions that have remained the same.

An ayahuasca ceremony is usually held during nighttime. Before the ceremony begins, the ceremonial space will be blessed and prepared by the shaman, whereafter the brew will be offered to the participants of the ceremony, depending on its nature. The brew might even be split into a few doses in some cases. The ceremony will last until the effects of the brew have worn off. The shaman's task is to provide guidance to those going through the ayahuasca 'experience,' as not all individuals who ingest the brew have a good or enlightening one. Some people experience a high level of panic, fear, and anxiety, and it is also not unheard of that an individual can have a good experience on one occasion, followed by a bad one during the next. The shaman is responsible for the safety of all participants in the ceremony and for the desired outcome of whatever the purpose of the ceremony was (Kubala, 2019).

Two omnipresent uses or purposes are evident in the indigenous use of ayahuasca. The first purpose is for spiritual healing ceremonies, and the other is for physical healing. During a healing ceremony, the shaman and their patient will both consume the brew, and its purging effect will cause them to vomit and experience diarrhea, which they believe rids them of worms and any other form of parasites that may cause illness. On the other hand, shamans, both ancient and modern, tend to use ayahuasca for practicing divination. The shaman would typically be visited by someone who wants to put a curse on someone, or similarly, they need a curse that was placed on them to be broken. Divination or sorcery, however, is similar to what is considered black magic and is not a common practice among all shamans. In many of these ceremonies, it would be the shaman who drinks the brew, and the individual who is consulting them would not be included. The reason for this is because the shaman is the one who is consulting spiritual beings and dealing with the energy of the curse, so they put themselves under the influence of the brew, working on behalf of the individual who consulted them.

This mind-altering magic brew eventually made its way to the Western World when the Spanish and Portuguese missionaries traveled to South America in the mid-1700s. According to one Jesuit by the name Franz Xavier Veigl, the natives in South America concocted a brew that serves the purpose of bewitching and mystifying the drinker. However, the presence of ayahuasca stayed relatively under wraps until the next century, where the rest of Europe caught wind of this magical tea. Explorers, such as the botanist Richard Spruce, traveled back to South America in the mid-1800s, to the Amazon, in order to study the flora of the forest, and more specifically, the plants used in the ayahuasca brew. However, the real ayahuasca rush in the Western world began in the 1960s, and people started streaming down to South America in search of the fabled gateway to the spirit world. The first book about the plants used in the ayahuasca brew was published in 1979 by Richard Evans Schultes, an ethnobotanist. The book is called *The Plants of the Gods: Their Sacred, Healing, and Hallucinogenic Properties*. After his work became more well-known, it only served to fuel the curiosity behind ayahuasca's mystical properties even more (Reality Sandwich, 2019).

The Westernization of Ayahuasca

Today's Western society travels to South America to participate in what is known as "ayahuasca tourism," where they take part in these ceremonies in order to find meaning in their own lives that have been consumed by materialism and a sense of shallow aimlessness. Thus, individuals who tend to participate in ayahuasca tourism tend to generally be wealthy professionals with higher education that seek a form of treatment that would provide longer-lasting results than pharmaceutical antidepressants, among other commonly prescribed western medicine. This current use of ayahuasca stands in stark contrast to its traditional use and purpose by indigenous peoples.

Taking the traditional brew and its original culture from the Amazon and South American continent, and bringing it to the colonized West, not to mention ultimately Westernizing its use and the underlying philosophy, has angered indigenous shamans who feel that their culture has been stolen from them. The West, doing what it does best, is even moving itself into the Amazon by opening ayahuasca retreats where Westerners, also known as "spiritual tourists," can go to have this otherworldly experience for reasons unrelated to its traditional use. These centers are not owned or managed by natives; however, some of them do employ traditional and indigenous shamans. Others will often have white shamans who acquired their skills by learning from an indigenous shaman. This development in the Amazon has a double-edged sword effect as, while the indigenous forests are being destroyed to construct these retreats, the surrounding villages are able to earn an income from the fact that the area has become a tourist hotspot.

For those who cannot travel to Central or South America, there are also similar retreat centers in other parts of the world that offer the same 'experience,' hence indigenous shamans are justified in feeling that ayahuasca is being taken from their homes in the Amazon. Alternatively, there are those who feel that spreading the benefits of ayahuasca is a positive act that brings its healing benefits to more people. Both viewpoints are understandable. Nevertheless, the plants used to make the brew no longer grow solely in the Amazon; today, they are also cultivated in other parts of the world. As the Amazon's natural forestland and territory is on a systematic decline due to urbanization and harmful deforestation, some argue this is a method of sustainability—to keep these special plants alive and growing.

Studies and Interesting Findings
The Church of Santo Daime

Ayahuasca was first implemented as part of a religious ritual in the Santo Daime Church, which is known as a forest-based religion that originated during the 1920s and '30s in the Amazon. The founder of the Church was known as Master Irineu, and he used the brew as part of a ritual in church ceremonies to unite different religious and spiritual beliefs, including indigenous, Catholic, esoteric, Caboclo, and spiritist beliefs. Not long after the implementation of this church, word spread, this practice gained in popularity, and those with specific interest regarding conducting communion using ayahuasca started to make themselves known.

This denomination still exists today, and members of this church still use ayahuasca as part of their sacramental communion. The recipe used to make the brew is very specific and is always prepared using the same method. Thus, the members of these congregations use ayahuasca in the context of a ritual considered relevant to their specific religion.

Clinical Studies: Ayahuasca and Drug Addiction

Addictive behavior has become so prevalent in society, with no sure-fire way to curb or cure it, that researchers have started looking in the direction of alternative methods for the development of new treatments and possible cures. One of those alternative options is making use of ayahuasca, and clinical studies have been conducted to test its potential on reducing addictive behavior in individuals with the tendency to form codependent habits. There has been a renewed interest in all psychedelic substances for their potential to support and alleviate symptoms, such as addiction and other mental health-related diagnoses, and several clinical trials have been conducted on ayahuasca's specific effect on addiction.

The inspiration for a clinical study on ayahuasca and its effects on drug and alcohol addiction in 2014 came from a long-term study on Brazilian churchgoers who use ayahuasca in their church ceremonies. This study indicated that, after individuals started using ayahuasca during these church ceremonies, their other addictive behavior started to decline and disappear. Researchers are aiming to create clinical studies that contain improved research methodologies, clinical protocols that are well-planned, and proper follow-ups, end-points, and proper controls.

In a study that looked at the neuropsychopharmacological and the long-term effects of ayahuasca on drug addiction, ayahuasca was administered to participants in a controlled, laboratory environment. Participants were healthy volunteers who were administered a dry, capsule-version of ayahuasca. This form of ayahuasca was made by following the traditional recipe using both the *B. caapi* and *P. viridis* plants to make the brew, but the ayahuasca was thereafter lyophilized, meaning that the brew was freeze-dried so it could be accurately dosed and placed in capsules. Normally, DMT alone would provide no psychedelic experience if ingested, as the stomach and liver's naturally inherent MAOIs destroy and digest this component. However, with the *B. caapi* mixed with the DMT-containing *P. viridis* in this capsule form, the participants would still be able to experience the effects of the DMT. The combination of this mix in the capsule mimics the experience as if they were consuming the brew. The other positives to lyophilization include that researchers can use standardized dosing and the use of placebos for a more accurate experiment and outcome expectation.

The dosage was quantified as follows: doses ranging between 0.5 mg and 1 mg per 1 kg of a participant's body weight were administered. In order to describe or characterize the subjective effects of the DMT/ayahuasca dose, the visual analog scales (VAS), the Hallucinogen Rating Scale (HRS), and the Addiction Research Center Inventory (ARCI) are consulted.

By applying these three tools along with the administration of the DMT/ayahuasca, a pattern containing certain characteristics started to become clear. At a neurophysiological level, researchers were able to identify spontaneous electrical activity in the brain when under the influence of ayahuasca, with a shift in energy distribution that shows higher on the electroencephalography (EEG) scale. This indicates higher frequencies within the brain. Researchers also noticed that activity in certain parts of the brain was modified when the patients were under the influence of ayahuasca, and when the participants reached the peak of their hallucinogenic experience, the cortical and paralimbic areas of the brain were activated. These areas of the brain relate to memory, cognitive control, and emotions. The same effects were observed in a study where ayahuasca was used to research sleep architecture.

Researchers have also consulted neo shamans who specialize in the treatment of addiction with ayahuasca and medical practitioners and were told that the therapeutic potential that helps treat addiction most likely comes from the visions the individual experiences when they are under the influence of the psychedelic component. Another important component, which is known as the somatic component, the *purga*, or throwing up after ingesting the substance, is seen as a type of cleansing procedure that is deemed as a crucial part of the overall therapeutic process. Patients who have to endure this purging symptom do not only get rid of unwanted toxins in their body but also believe that they are benefitting from a more metaphorical type of internal cleansing that increases the effectiveness of the treatment by expelling unwanted mental components.

The study concluded that not only were there significant decreases in the participants' addictive behavior, but the ayahuasca also appeared to soothe other negative or self-destructive behavior resembling obsessive-compulsive behavior and impulsivity. Finally, they observed that there was a significant positive change in participants' sense of "self-directedness" (Bouso & Riba, 2014).

Ayahuasca Can Help You Grow New Brain Cells

When it comes to drugs, and most people tend to place all of them in the same basket, you have most likely heard someone, somewhere say, "man, people should stop doing drugs—they're gonna lose all of their brain cells!" This is exactly why all substances should not be classified as "drugs"—this word is highly stigmatized. For example, after reading most of this book, we hope you find it is clear that psilocybin cannot be compared to crack cocaine. This study from the Beckley Foundation shows us exactly why we can't just refer to *every* mind-body altering substance as a drug and place them all within this same stigmatized concept.

For quite a long time, despite ongoing scientific and neurological research, medical experts believed that an adult brain cannot create new brain cells or neurons. This would implicate that, when you get older, your brain cells die and are not replaced by new ones. Only later, the phenomenon of neurogenesis was discovered, which means the creation of new neurons does in fact take place in the brain, and scientists could determine that this occurs in the hippocampus region. Coincidence or not, the hippocampus is also associated with our ability to form memories. Even though this was a spectacular discovery, scientists also realized that neurogenesis does not necessarily work fast enough to be able to maintain brain health and replace all damaged neurons, especially as one gets older. The consequences of neurogenesis not being able to keep up with the eventual degeneration of cells as we age can result in conditions, like dementia, and other neurodegenerative conditions, like Alzheimer's disease. The Beckley Foundation study, which focuses on the effects that ayahuasca has on neurogenesis, was conducted by the Beckley/Sant Pau Research Programme and is published in the reputable journal, *Scientific Reports*. The basic outcome of the study is that there are specific compounds within the ayahuasca brew that stimulate neurogenesis—the birth or creation of new and fresh neurons ready to rumble! How did researchers find this out, though?

They looked at neural cells and were interested in two specific substances in order to test their effects on cell growth. They were specifically interested in two compounds present in ayahuasca, namely harmine and tetrahydroharmine, which are the two most prominent alkaloids found in the ayahuasca brew. Researchers placed hippocampal stem cells in a petri dish along with the two alkaloids, and according to their observations, the rate at which the young cells matured into fully-developed neurons were much higher than normal. Not only did this mean that ayahuasca has neurogenic properties, but it also opens up a wealth of possibilities regarding ayahuasca's use in the treatment of neural conditions (Beckley Foundation, 2017).

The Benefits of Ayahuasca Backed by Research

1. Ayahuasca can improve your psychological well being.

   Research conducted on how ayahuasca influences brain activity has shown that taking the brew can increase one's ability to approach life mindfully—meaning being present in the moment and more aware of one's surroundings. Not only can it increase this capacity in your mind, but it can also improve overall components of one's psychological wellness. Studies indicate that taking ayahuasca can improve mindfulness, mood, and the regulation of emotions. This is shown in a study where 20 participants consumed ayahuasca once a week for four weeks and compared its effectiveness to the same as participating in a week-long mindfulness program. After the trials, their sense of acceptance was significantly increased. Acceptance is one of the components of the mindfulness practice that plays an underlying role in mental health (Kubala, 2019).

2. Ayahuasca can assist in the treatment of anxiety, PTSD, and depression, all of which are generally considered treatment-resistant.

   Several studies have been conducted to indicate ayahuasca's potential in the treatment of this variety of debilitating conditions.

- A study that involved 29 participants all suffering from treatment-resistant depression indicated that administering a single dose of ayahuasca showed a significant and rapid improvement in the severity of their symptoms.

- A review of six studies further lays the foundation that ayahuasca is a beneficial treatment method for anxiety, depression, mood disorders, drug addiction, and depression.

- There are several studies conducted on ayahuasca's optimistic effects on addiction disorders, which included addiction to alcohol, crack cocaine, and nicotine, wherein all three cases' positive results were noted.

- Another study involved 12 participants who were each having issues with substance abuse. They participated in a 4-day treatment program with two ayahuasca ceremonies. A six-month follow-up procedure was conducted where these participants showed great signs of improvement that manifested in the form of mindfulness, a sense of empowerment, a sense of hope for the future, and an increased quality of life. Participants also reported that their addictive behavior had declined significantly.

- PTSD is also being researched with regards to ayahuasca as a treatment option; however, this method needs further research (Kubala, 2019).

Big Pharma and the Banning of Ayahuasca

Figuring out the legal status of ayahuasca, especially in its countries of origin, can be complicated due to the fact that it is used for religious purposes. This forms a grey area, legally speaking, especially since it has an extensive history of indigenous religious use and plays a significant role in indigenous religious ceremonies.

In the United States, the psychedelic compound DMT, which is present in ayahuasca, is classified as a Schedule 1 substance. However, rulings by the Supreme Court and exceptions granted by the Drug Enforcement Administration led to exceptions related to the use of ayahuasca in specific cases that are protected by the concept of religious freedom. Here are some of the most recent incidents and information regarding the legality of ayahuasca in the United States:

1. Ayahuasca, due to its containing the Schedule 1 substance DMT, is illegal to sell, consume, import, and distribute in the United States.

2. Two churches have been granted exemption from this rule and are allowed to use ayahuasca during their communion or church ceremonies. The first of these churches is União do Vegetal, or the UDV, which became involved in a tense federal court case. We break this down in the following section. The second church is the previously mentioned Santo Daime, which has several congregations in the United States—located in Washington, Oregon, California, and Massachusetts.

3. The maximum statutory punishment for the unlicensed possession of DMT or a DMT containing substance is 20 years in prison. This would then include ayahuasca (ICEERS, 2019).

The Story of Gonzales v. O Centro Espírita Beneficente União do Vegetal

Uniao Do Vegetal is one of the churches that exist in the United States that uses ayahuasca during their religious ceremonies. Or, as they call it, *hoasca*. As we now know, ayahuasca goes by many names. On May 21st, 1999, agents from the U.S. Customs Department entered the church's national headquarters and took all existing church records, including devices that could contain records, like computers, and all of the supplies of the church's hoasca tea that was stored there.

After about 18 months of unsuccessful attempts to negotiate some kind of settlement with the government which would ultimately support or accommodate the traditional religious practices of UDV, the religious institution filed a lawsuit against the DEA in federal court. However, they not only targeted the DEA, but they also took issue with the U.S. Customs Service and the United States Department of Justice for violating the First Amendment of the Constitution, several treaty obligations, and the Religious Freedom Restoration Act (Centro Espírita Beneficente União Do Vegetal, 2020).

Fundamentally, the UDV sought relief under the Religious Freedom Restoration Act (RFRA) of 1993. This act prohibits the U.S. government from interfering with religious acts or conduct unless it can prove to a court that there is a "compelling interest" that supports the cause, and also that the government will be using the "least restrictive means" in doing so. If the government is unable to follow this protocol, it cannot legally interfere with any specific religious practice.

The U.S. government responded to the lawsuit by claiming that it had a compelling interest regarding limiting the use of controlled substances and that the only way their compelling interest could be addressed was by implementing a full ban without any exceptions. With this statement, they implied that the UDV's use of hoasca was to be included in this ban. The government's argument was that the use of hoasca during religious ceremonies put the UDV's members at risk; however, lawyers for UDV argued that this is speculative, and cannot measure up against years of research and empirical evidence gathered about ayahuasca. Furthermore, the evidence presented in the court indicated that the quantity of DMT present in the hoasca tea used by the UDV church is small and can be compared to amounts of DMT that are present in other plants growing in the United States. Their evidence also referenced that DMT has been found naturally present in a healthy human body, specifically the brain.

Ultimately, the use and purpose of hoasca in the UDV religious ceremonies were compared by the Tenth Circuit Court of Appeals as similar to the use of peyote in bona fide religious ceremonies conducted by the Native American Church, which is considered legitimate by Congress and is not a criminalized act according to the Controlled Substances Act. The ruling, in short, states that,

> *"União do Vegetal's use of hoasca occurs in a 'traditional, precisely circumscribed ritual' where the drug 'itself is an object of worship,' and using the sacrament outside the religious context is a sacrilege"* (Centro Espírita Beneficente União Do Vegetal, 2020).

In other words, because this religious institution regards the recreational use of hoasca as a sacrilege, it is similar to the use of peyote by the Native American Church, which is also permitted by the Controlled

Substances Act. We'll cover this topic in more depth in the following chapter.

However, government defendants appealed the case to the US Supreme Court on February 10th, 2005. The reason for the appeal was that the defendants were not willing to accept any of the prior court rulings, nor Congress' passage of the RFRA, which were all in favor of UDV using hoasca during their religious ceremonies. Their attempts were futile, however; on April 18th, 2005, the Supreme Court heard the case of *Gonzales v. O Centro Espírita Beneficente União do Vegetal*, and on February 21st, 2006, the United States Supreme Court ruled unanimously, resulting in the affirmation of UDV's religious freedom (Centro Espírita Beneficente União Do Vegetal, 2020).

After the results of the UDV Supreme Court case, the DEA implemented certain procedures under Congressionally-granted authority that allows the importation and the distribution of ayahuasca only under license. Unlicensed importation and distribution will still be regarded as a felony under both federal and state law.

Ayahuasca Today

When taking ayahuasca, several things happen inside your body. Remember that this also depends on how strong the brew is that you are consuming. The first, unpleasant side effect will be vomiting or diarrhea, and you can also expect to experience a temporary period of panic, paranoia, or anxiety. This brief bout of anxiety is considered normal, although the individual experiencing it can find it extremely frightening. After ingesting Ayahuasca, it will increase your heart rate and blood pressure, so if you are on medication for these reasons, you should not consume this brew.

While you are under the influence, your life and your safety are in the hands of the shaman who leads the ceremony, as they are the ones who know the ingredients of the brew as well as the dosage of each ingredient (Kubala, 2019).

Apart from your body, there are interesting things happening in your brain when you are under the influence of ayahuasca. The brew causes vivid visual hallucinatory experiences for those who consume it, and fascinated researchers in the United Kingdom conducted a study on the brain by measuring its electrical activity while under the influence of ayahuasca. The study, conducted at the *Imperial College London Centre for Psychedelic Research* in 2019, was published in the journal, *Scientific Reports,* and it involved neural assessment while administering ayahuasca intravenously to participants.

The research methodology included recruiting 13 healthy participants, who received the drug intravenously, as compared with the administration of a placebo. Each participant was fitted with a cap that used electrodes to capture EEG activity before, during, and after they had received the dose. Researchers found that when ayahuasca was administered, there was a drop in alpha waves. Alpha waves are the fundamental electrical waves in the brain when an individual is awake. An increase in theta waves was also noticed—theta waves are fundamentally present when we are dreaming.

These are not the only observations, though. Researchers noted that there were indications of new frequencies or "rhythmicity," and researchers are postulating that this may point to another type of brain activity instead of only the normal indication of sleep. Overall, researchers described brain activity as being more chaotic, and they were confident that the changes in brain activity were unique from those observed when a participant is under the influence of other psychedelics, like LSD or psilocybin.

Researchers describe the brain activity as indicative that the participants are wholly immersed in their experiences, and they liken it to daydreaming, only on a whole new level considering its vividness and how immersed each participant is in the experience. One of the leading researchers, Christopher Timmermann, who is a Ph.D. candidate in neuropsychology at the Imperial College London, likened it to "dreaming with your eyes open" (Mammoser, 2019b). A professor in neuroscience, Draulio Araujo from the *Brain Institute, Federal University of Rio Grande do Norte* (UFRN) in Natal, Brazil, has further hypothesized that the state can be likened more to dreaming than hallucinating. Araujo, who also holds a Ph.D., has extensively studied the effects of ayahuasca on the brain.

Need-To-Know Information About Ayahuasca Use

We know now that after ingesting ayahuasca, you're going to experience some adverse effects, traditionally known as *purga*. To make things a bit easier for you, avoid consuming the following list of foods before taking part in an ayahuasca ceremony:

- chocolate
- sauerkraut
- herring

- anchovies
- any cured meats
- aged cheeses
- fermented sausage
- fava beans
- any caffeinated beverages
- alcohol
- caviar
- chicken or beef liver
- yogurt

Do you see a pattern of fermented foods here? They may cause a very unpleasant experience. It's best to avoid these foods for at least two weeks before taking part in an ayahuasca ceremony.

Next, after the ingestion and the purge, what will you most likely experience when the ayahuasca brew takes over? There's a long list of interesting feelings and emotions that may cross your psychedelic path. They include the following:

- physical aches and pains
- an altered sense of time and space
- paranoia, anxiety, and fear
- a difficulty balancing or standing upright
- a complete sensation of being overwhelmed
- auditory hallucinations

- a sedative state
- euphoria
- intense feelings of love and empathy
- deep feelings of acceptance of the self and of others
- spiritual experiences that can be life-altering
- inner peace
- a sense of mental therapy
- a loss of one's ego
- a feeling of being connected to the universe
- visual hallucinations, both when eyes are open and closed
- feeling chilly and sweaty.

These symptoms are considered normal. However, there are also adverse effects that you should know about. Ingesting ayahuasca can carry the risk of developing PTSD and HPPD, which stands for Hallucinogen Persisting Perception Disorder, where the user's vision is distorted by experiencing an effect that looks like snow in their vision. These effects can easily be avoided by making sure the necessary preparation is done, proper guidance is provided during a ritual, and by ensuring proper integration.

In the end, ayahuasca is not an exotic hallucinogenic from the Amazon anymore, although that will always be its history and heritage. It has morphed into a multifaceted and miraculous healing aid—a secret that has been known by indigenous shamans for centuries (Reality Sandwich, 2019).

CHAPTER 5: ALL-NATURAL AYAHUASCA

Dosage Guide

An ayahuasca dosage is usually determined by the shaman who prepares the brew. However, if you are curious about how much of the hallucinogenic plant to use, the table below contains the ingredients of a recipe that provides one serving of ayahuasca.

Hallucinogenic ingredients	• 5–10g acacia root bark (*Mimosa hostilis*) • 2–5 grams of Syrian rue seeds (powdered)
Non-hallucinogenic ingredients	• 1–2 eggs • White vinegar (distilled)

(PsychonautWiki, 2021)

Chapter 6:
What's Inside Peyote?

Peyote can be seen as ayahuasca's North American cousin as it has a long history in parts of this continent regarding spiritual use, and even for the healing of physical ailments. Peyote contains a different hallucinogenic compound called mescaline. This interesting part of Native American culture also holds some secrets to health improvements, be they mental or physical. The publication *Nature* described peyote as follows:

> *"Peyote contains from four to seven remarkable alkaloids, one of which is capable of causing colored hallucinations. With eyes closed, the fortunate worshipper may, for hours, enjoy a kaleidoscopic play of the most indescribably beautiful visions of geometric figures and familiar things on a background of constantly changing colors so exquisitely rich as to seem supernatural. It is easy to understand, then, how such a powerful plant could be regarded as a "messenger" capable of putting the individual in communication with the gods without the medium of a priest, for peyote is believed by members of the cult to form such a function. (Schultes 1937, 155)"* (Dyck & Bradford, 2012).

What is Peyote?

Peyote can be described as a smaller type of cactus that appears spineless. It's scientifically known as *Lophophora williamsii*, and it contains a high concentration of mescaline, which gives it its potent psychedelic powers. Peyote is native only to certain parts of North and MesoAmerica, including Mexico and Southwestern Texas, in the Coahuila, Chihuahuan Desert, Tamaulipas, Nuevo León, and San Luis Potosí.

According to archeological studies, there are indications that peyote has been used by Native Americans for more than 5500 years. Native American tribes living in Oklahoma, Texas, and Mexico in past times, used peyote for healing and spiritual enlightenment. Tribes like the Tarahumara and Chichimeca are even known for using Peyote to ease the pain in their feet after long periods of walking for long-distance migrations.

Deconstructing Peyote

Lophophora williamsii is a cactus that grows very slowly—so slow that it takes about 10-30 years for the plant to reach full maturity. After this blue-green, hairy plant is fully matured, it will produce flowers; it can also develop a pink fruit that is edible after the flowering phase. The fact that a peyote plant takes so long to grow makes it a rarity, and if one can imagine the level of popularity mescaline has reached in the West through the years, these plants are now considered to be at risk according to standard NatureServe conservation guidelines. Peyote is known for containing a wide range of alkaloids, but its primary psychedelic component is mescaline. Mescaline's hallucinogenic effect is similar to that one would get from LSD and psilocybin, lasting several hours—mostly between 4 and 8 hours. When ingesting mescaline-containing peyote, one can expect to experience a distorted sense of time and space, open and closed-eyed visuals, and what can be described as an altered thought process.

Peyote doesn't really taste very nice, and there are two methods of preparation for consumption—one is preferred over the other, especially by Westerners who may not be specifically looking for a specific or premeditated spiritual experience, or who are not used to its taste. In the first method of preparation, the top part of the cactus is dried and then eaten. Alternatively, it can be crushed into a liquid slush which is then drunk. The levels of mescaline remaining in the peyote differs between the two methods as fresh peyote only contains about 0.4% mescaline. However, if the peyote is dried, the mescaline level goes up to 3–6%. That's quite a difference.

During Native American religious ceremonies, the participants are allowed to consume fresh peyote legally. However, it is mostly consumed dried, and due to its horrible bitter taste, people tend to consume as little as possible in order to get the effects they want. Take note that going on a peyote-hunting expedition, and attempting to prepare and consume it without guidance, can be dangerous as these cacti have varying alkaloid levels, and you may identify the wrong cactus, which can be harmful to consume.

Peyote and its Many Names

The name 'Peyote' as we know it comes from an ancient Aztec word *peyōtl*, which, when translated, means "divine messenger." There are also other names for Peyote which are linked to its hallucinogenic compound. These include Mescalito, Mescaline, and Buttons. The name "Buttons" refers to the part of the cactus which is used for consumption—the top part.

As we now know, the scientific name for peyote is *Lophophora williamsii*. *Lophophora*, the genus, also has other species apart from *williamsii* like *koehresii*, *williamsii var*, *caespitosa*, *diffusa*, *fricii*, and *jourdaniana*. The *Lophophora* genus can be easily identified by looking for its button-like appearance, as well as the fact that these cacti have no spines. Peyote is thus easy to identify as they are small, hairy, have a button-like appearance, and have white-petaled flowers if they are in their mature stage. Their flowering season is between the months of March and May, so if you're going to be looking for white flowers in November, even on a mature Peyote, you're not going to have any luck.

History, and Traditional Use

Peyote has been peacefully growing in the Southwestern parts of North America and Mexico since the dawn of time, and evidence of human use and consumption suggests that its cultural use dates back more than 5000 years. There is little knowledge of the indigenous cultures who used this cactus so long ago as most traces of them have vanished. Archeological evidence does suggest that peyote was definitely used in ritualistic ceremonies or rites during these pre-ancient times.

The indigenous use of Peyote can also be traced back to the Tonkawa and Mescalero tribes in New Mexico and Texas. While peyote was originally associated with these tribes in the southern parts of North America, other tribes like the Cora, Chichimeca, Tarahumara, and Huichol tribes were also known for using peyote.

As with ayahuasca, the first Westerners who made contact with peyote were the Spaniards early in the sixteenth century when they conquered Mexico. One of the first mentions of peyote is in friar Bernardino de Sahagún, a scholar of the time's study called *The General History of the Things of New Spain,* from 1529. Spanish missionaries, who observed the effects of the mescaline on those who ingested it thought it to be abhorrent, and they attempted to suppress its use in what was then called "New Spain" (modern-day Mexico). Their attempts were not successful. On the contrary, the use of peyote spread to Native Americans, like the Osage Nation, who were living in the Southwestern parts of the United States, and who were, during that time, forced into reservations. (Abbott, 2019).

Between this period and the twentieth century, the use and effects of mescaline did not spread as widely as ayahuasca did, and only a few attempted to sample the mysterious cactus apart from those of the Native American cultures. However, those who did try the substance reported new interest in this plant for recreational, medicinal, and spiritual use. During that time, it was known that one has to toughen up before taking mescaline as, in contrast to alcohol, it gives a nasty hangover before it starts to work its magic.

The First Experimental Ventures

What makes mescaline use interesting is that Native American cultures seemed to have some knowledge of how to obtain consistent results from the cactus after ingesting it. When others, including Westerners, tried peyote, they would have more unpredictable experiences, which were in some cases very unpleasant. For example, a physician John Raleigh Briggs, from Texas, decided to test mescaline by taking a small bite from a dried button in 1887. He reported experiencing "rather violent symptoms," including having difficulty breathing and a racing heart. Nevertheless, the Detroit-based pharmaceutical company Parke-Davis in Michigan decided to start experimenting with the mescaline component in peyote as cocaine was no longer an option after its adverse effects had been revealed. They were looking for a drug of botanical origin, and in 1893, the company started marketing peyote infusions for respiratory issues and as a heart tonic (Abbott, 2019).

The release of these tonics inspired a whirlwind of new scientific studies. During this time, safety and ethics regards were not high on the priority list, and scientists used themselves or other subjects for testing. Two reports that clearly showed the unpredictability of the mescaline were published in 1895 at the academic institution now known as George Washington University in Washington D.C. In one study, two scientists administered the substance to a 24-year-old man, which resulted in paranoia and delusion. In the other study, a chemist chewed peyote buttons, the number of which is unknown, and developed pleasant visions that he felt he had control over; but what followed was 18 hours of depression and severe insomnia.

While all of this was happening in Washington D.C., William Maloney and Alwyn Knauer, both New York City pharmacologists, decided to conduct a larger trial in 1913 on 23 participants. Their hypothesis was that mescaline would give them more insight into the inner workings of a schizophrenic's mind. However, this failed spectacularly. As they recorded each participant's behavior and communications while they were hallucinating, they could ultimately find no link between any of the participants' behaviors when under the influence of mescaline. An interesting fact that was later discovered, is that schizophrenic patients have the ability to discern between hallucinations caused by their illness and those induced by taking a hallucinogenic. For example, in a research study conducted on Schizophrenia and hallucinogens, schizophrenic patients who have taken hallucinogens before recounted the nature of the hallucinations as different than those typical of their illness.

A schizophrenic patient can, for example, experience visual hallucinations as part of their illness, although auditory hallucinations are more common. However, if these hallucinations were to be caused by a hallucinogenic drug, they will be able to identify this as the experience would not only be less "real," but hallucinogens overall produce positive experiences, while schizophrenic episodes do not. Schizophrenic patients are also prone to experiencing paranoid delusions; however, when under the influence of hallucinogenic drugs, they would mostly report somatic delusions. Even though hallucinogens affect the same neurotransmitters in the brain as those that are affected by Schizophrenia, the experience still seems different to patients who take hallucinogenic drugs. This can imply that psychedelics can be used to further study the nature and origin of a mental illness we know very little about, starting at this first key difference (Fairmount Behavioral Health System, 2021).

Eventually, synthetic mescaline was also developed and available for research purposes. The first chemist who was able to create a synthesized version was Austrian chemist, Ernst Späth, at the University of Vienna. It took the pharmaceutical company Merck—yes, that one!—less than a year to place synthesized mescaline on the market after its invention; however, synthesized mescaline did not provide any indication of more consistent results in testing or make trial outcomes more reliable (Abbott, 2019).

The focus on peyote shifted from botany to chemistry when Dr. John Raleigh Briggs conducted the first pharmacological study on peyote in North America. His experience is published in his work *Muscale Buttons'—Physiological Effects—Personal Experience in The Medical Register,* where he tells of his jumping pulse rate, emotional distress, and headaches. His encounter drew the attention of medical scientists and pharmacologists, and the scope of mescaline study has changed completely since that incident (Reality Sandwich, 2019a).

Peyote: From Recreational Use to Secret State Shenanigans

The small circle of individuals who knew about peyote and had access to it due to their artistic status in society was also having a spectacular time ingesting peyote to boost their creativity, to come up with new ideas, and to enjoy the bohemian lifestyle. There are quite a few interesting theories among the artists, writers, and philosophers' use of peyote—most of whom lived in the early twentieth century. Although not all of them used scientific methodology in their endeavors, the efforts are insightful not only by looking at the creative approaches and ideas of the users, but also by looking at the variety of situations after ingestion, and whether they found this method to be successful for them as artists and thinkers. Artists and other self-proclaimed bohemians were testing how peyote could enhance their creative ability in Europe, too. Not long after, local psychiatrists and other researchers got wind of these experiments and they started their own, specifically on creative types such as these philosophers, writers, and artists of mention.

- A British Surrealist artist named Julian Trevelyan found the ingestion of peyote inspiring for the creation of surrealist-themed paintings. Considering the hallucinogenic effect of peyote, this is understandable, as one would easily be able to visualize absurd and surrealist ideas after its ingestion.

- Another surrealist painter named Basil Beaumont, however, did not have the same fortune, as he experienced excruciating pain and fear while under the influence.

- The French nihilist and existentialist philosopher, Jean-Paul Sartre, entered what he described as a "grotesque hell" after ingesting peyote.

- The famous British writer and hedonist, Aldous Huxley, wrote in his 1954 work *The Doors of Perception* that, after he consumed the peyote, he was transported to a magnificent new world where he experienced an expansion of consciousness.

Mescaline was also used in experiments during World War II in the human experimentation program of the Third Reich. In this context, mescaline was seen as a possible 'veritaserum,' or truth serum, and Kurt Plötner, a Nazi physician, forced concentration camp victims to take mescaline for interrogation purposes, thinking that it would make them reveal unknown truths.

Even the CIA was testing mescaline as a truth serum during this same time. This hypothesis was soon abandoned, however, as the vomiting that followed the ingestion of the mescaline created an even more strained trust-relationship between the interrogator and the participants—they probably thought that they were being poisoned. Not long after, Project MK-Ultra was founded and Kurt Plötner was recruited by the CIA to take part in the research and experiments in this mind-control venture. The founding of Project MK-Ultra also indicated a new ruler in the realm of psychedelic research—LSD (Abbott, 2019).

One of the biggest issues with peyote research seems to be the fact that there was a constant lack of consistency in the results. This would make further studies a waste of time as inconsistency in a possible medical treatment or substance cannot be placed on the market as a viable treatment option. What are the treatment potentials for peyote, if any?

Studies and Interesting Findings

In comparison to ayahuasca, there are fewer trials where researchers use peyote, and the therapeutic focus of this substance appears to be addiction therapy.

The Preservation and Sustainability of Peyote

As we know, these curious little cacti take a long time to mature, and now that their effects have become known to such a wide chunk of the global population, they have been overharvested for years and years. This caused them to become an addition to the endangered species list. There are proper ways to harvest peyote that ensures the development of a new plant. However, improper harvesting is a common practice and leads to the destruction of the plant and its inability to form a new replacement. In essence, improper harvesting destroys the root structure of the plant, which then makes reproduction impossible. There are many societies who are cultivating this plant with the hopes to keep the species alive, and the rule of thumb for using sacred plants that is generally followed is that, for each plant harvested and consumed, three must be planted as a replacement. One of the biggest challenges is the fact that this plant does not easily adapt to any climate or soil, and it only grows in a very small part of the Americas.

An even bigger threat that can lead to the destruction of this plant species today is the operation of drug cartels and mining operations that are eyeing sacred sites currently protected by UNESCO. In Mexico, for example, the mining of silver has destroyed an area where peyote used to grow, and while this creates jobs and income for the residents in the area, it puts the plant's existence in danger (Seer, 2017).

The Appeal of Peyote

The Appeal of Peyote is a book authored by Dr. Richard Evans Schultes about the medicinal properties of this curious plant. According to Schultes, peyote can be used for an extensive list of ailments, which includes congestion, headaches, arthritis, knee pain, and fatigue. If used in microdoses, it can also alleviate sensations of both hunger and thirst, which was a useful tool for Native American tribes who traveled long distances on foot in areas often scarce of food and water. Another physician, Dr. Stacey Schaefer, also supports the hypothesis of peyote containing antibiotic properties. Furthermore, her professional opinion is that peyote has the ability to increase human growth hormones (HGH) and that it shows a positive immune response to malignant or cancerous tumors in the body. Schaefer says that these are enough reasons to classify peyote as medicine.

Another medical researcher, Dr. John Halpern, found that peyote can be used as a therapeutic treatment for addictive disorders like alcohol and drug addiction. Apart from this, Halpern also states that peyote can be used to treat depression and anxiety. Not only is it incredibly difficult to find any sources of medical trials where peyote is used, the government's reasons for outlawing a substance that carries so much potential according to these medical professionals is also a question worthy of consideration (Seer, 2017).

Peyote as an Antibiotic

There are preliminary studies that indicate peyote's antibiotic properties. The preliminary study was conducted on mice who suffered from a staph infection but were resistant to penicillin. Mice that were given no treatment all died within 60 hours, while mice that received treatment that contained peyote all survived. These studies were conducted at the Department of Bacteriology at the University of Arizona (Reality Sandwich, 2019a).

Big Pharma and the Banning of Peyote

Peyote is currently listed as a Schedule 1 substance by the Comprehensive Drug Abuse Prevention and Control Act, which makes its use illegal in the United States. The only exception is for religious ceremonial use by the Native American Church, according to the American Indian Religious Freedom Act. A 1994 amendment of this act also protects the harvesting, consumption, and cultivation of peyote for religious ceremonies.

Peyote is not listed or regulated by Article 32 of the Convention on Psychotropic Substances, which was passed in 1971 by the United Nations.

You can find some legally in Canada though, as it is pointedly exempt from the Controlled Drugs and Substances Act. This means that possession is legal, but it is not permitted to grow the cacti for consumption purposes. Canada wants you to grow them for ornamental purposes only. If you don't want peyote as an ornament specifically, I suggest you visit Ukraine, where it is legal to possess, cultivate, and transport it.

In the United Kingdom, cacti that have hallucinogenic components are legal unless they are in a state where they have been prepared for consumption (Reality Sandwich, 2019a).

The American Indian Religious Freedom Act

Native American religious practices using peyote were prohibited because peyote, or mescaline, was classified as a Schedule 1 drug. Thus, they could practice their ceremonies; however, the use of peyote was illegal. This is the basis of the development of the American Indian Religious Freedom Act, which also inspired the freedom to use ayahuasca in religious ceremonies by two specific churches. This law is also abbreviated as AIRFA and is now a United States federal law that was enacted by a joint resolution in 1978 of the Congress. Before this enactment, Native American sacred rituals and ceremonies were prohibited and seen as a federal offense.

This law returned civil rights not only to Native Americans, but also to Inuit, Aleuts, and Native Hawaiians. This act protects these groups' inherent rights to have freedom of belief and freedom of expression, and protects their ability to exercise their traditional religious rites and cultural practices, whether or not it includes the use of a psychedelic substance. It also protects their rights to be in possession of objects that are traditionally considered to be sacred within their cultures. The act requires the U.S. government to cease any interference with Native American religious practices, and this specification is based on the requirements of the First Amendment of the United States Constitution.

There were three main areas of conflict that supported the Native American Church's position in this matter.

1. The passing of the General Allotment Acts and the Indian Removal Act caused the forced displacement and relocation of many Native American tribes and families. For example, most people from the Five Civilized Tribes were forced to live in the Central Plains in the United States, and Native American tribes and societies were ultimately removed from their sacred lands where they held their traditional ceremonies just like their ancestors did. The significance behind this is that Native American spiritual culture is bound to its location, which means that there are now some ceremonies and rituals that cannot and have not been performed for a very long time.

2. There are other exceptions made for Native Americans to be able to practice their culture and to possess items that they deem sacred. For example, eagles are considered an endangered species in the United States; yet, exceptions are made for the hunting of eagles by Native Americans. So, what makes peyote any different if it is also seen as sacred and necessary for ceremonial purposes?
3. Finally, from a legal perspective, the government is not supposed to interfere with the religious practices of a specific group, unless they have very good reasons to do so, and if they can do this in a non-disruptive manner. This directly points to the fact that Native Americans did not receive equal treatment under the law and their sacred rituals and ceremonies were often a source for interference by government officials.

The AIRFA act thus not only acknowledges the prior injustice and infringement upon Native Americans' right to freedom of religion but also specifically their right to the free exercise of their beliefs (Vecsey, 1991).

President Jimmy Carter gave the following statement regarding the American Indian Religious Freedom Act:

> *"In the past, Government agencies and departments have on occasion denied Native Americans access to particular sites, and interfered with religious practices and customs where such use conflicted with Federal regulations. In many instances, the Federal officials responsible for the enforcement of these regulations were unaware of the nature of traditional native religious practices and, consequently, of the degree to which their agencies interfered with such practices"* (The American Presidency Project, 1978).

The Native American Church and Their Rights in Canada

Little is known or has been published about the Native American Church founded in the 19th century in Canada. They, just like their North American counterparts, also use peyote in their church ceremonies. After the establishment of the Native American Church in North America, peyote and its use started spreading from its Southwestern place of origin systematically up north until it reached Canada. In the early twentieth century, Canadian officials became aware of the use of peyote in Canada, and in the 1920s, there were several police reports indicating its use at a resort in Saskatchewan called Piapot. The peyote was allegedly brought into Canada by members of the Native American Church who had family residing in Dakota and Montana. It was via the migration of the peyote from the Northern parts of the United States over the Canadian border that made Canadian officials acquainted with both peyote and the Native American Church at that time. In fact, for most of three decades spanning from the 1920s to the 1940s, Canadian officials did not suspect that the transport of peyote over the Canadian border had anything to do with an established community within Canada that was using it; in contrast, they thought that every incident was due to US-specific conditions.

Things changed when an Australian anthropologist contacted the Department of Indian Affairs in 1932 as they were looking for more information about the alleged use of peyote in British Columbia. This inquiry from the anthropologist appeared to catch local authorities off-guard, and Federal Bureaucrats immediately started sending correspondence to local agents inquiring about this controversial statement. Local agents assured them, however, that there was no peyote used under their watch, and for a few years, everything went back to normal.

Into the 1940s, increasing surveillance, which was sometimes offered by local civilians, reignited the idea that peyote use was alive and well; but still, no solid evidence could be found. The Canadian government received a warning by a US doctor named Charles Tranter in 1942, who lived in Reno, Nevada. His correspondence told Canadian authorities that US authorities had noticed a significant rise in the use of peyote in Southern parts of the United States. Tranter created an image of intoxication, inefficiency, and cult-related behavior in his correspondence. He is quoted as saying:

> *"Indian peddlers bring the narcotic from Mexico, and it is used in all-night meetings. It has cut down the efficiency of our Indians approximately fifty percent in this region, and several deaths have occurred in the all-night meetings"* (Dyck & Bradford, 2012).

After three decades of mostly ignorance by Canadian officials, they started to pay more attention to the use of peyote by the mid-1950s. The initial suspicion was not in British Columbia where the first signs of peyote use were suggested, but on Alberta's Sunchild Cree Reserve, and also later in Saskatchewan, among members of the Red Pheasant band. Canadian officials have also changed their tune at this point, as they did not see the use of peyote as the source of Americans visiting Canada or as isolated incidents, but as a far more sustained part of the Native American Church and native bands in Canada. Authorities realized that the use of peyote had become an integral part of the religious practice of North American Aboriginal communities in Canada, especially on the Canadian prairies. Specifically, Nakoda, Cree, and other Aboriginal societies were claiming the substance for medicinal purposes and for the purpose of spiritual ceremonies. Subsequently, peyote became a subject of political debate, with many citizens feeling that the state should intervene in their use of what they perceived as an abhorrent and harmful substance.

Louis Sunchild emerged as a mentionable figure who advocated for the cultural and spiritual use of peyote. As a leader of his community at that time, he signed a treaty with the Canadian government in 1944 which led to the establishment of the Sunchild First Nation. However, he received negative attention from healthcare workers and the National Department of Health and Welfare when they expressed concerns that he acted in his own capacity as a healer or medicine man. A young girl who witnessed one of his rituals claimed that they were dangerous and that, during the ritual, Sunchild himself became a manifestation of the devil. On another occasion, there was an assault reported of a young girl. The perpetrators were alleged "members of the cult," which would be Sunchild's First Nation, and they were under the influence of peyote. This caused a split in the reserve, and several members decided to move as they did not want to participate in the activities anymore.

Incidents like these inspired headlines such as "Devil's Brew—or Sacred Potion?" Sunchild did his fair share of spreading not only the use of peyote but also his methodology of spiritual ceremonies across the indigenous or aboriginal peoples of Canada. Ultimately, the introduction of peyote created tension between the aboriginal-newcomer relations. Federal Bureaucrats were also in constant conflict with local police as they felt obliged to uphold the Native American Church's rights to use peyote as part of their religious ceremonies, while the police and Indian agents felt strongly that the use of the substance should be restricted on reserves. Ultimately, members of the Native American Church gave testimony that, if they were freely allowed to use peyote, which is sacred to them, as part of their rituals and ceremonies, this would ultimately have helped to heal deeper issues caused by colonialism (Dyck & Bradford, 2012).

Indigenous use of peyote remains alive and well, and the Native American Church uses peyote during their ceremonies, which has caused a more widespread use of the substance throughout North America. Peyote is still used in their religious practices today (Reality Sandwich, 2019a).

Peyote Today

Peyote is used by the Native American Church and in private ceremonies for healing, even though there is not a lot of scientific data that supports this kind of healing. However, there are individuals who have experience with peyote ceremonies, and their emphasis is always on mental preparation and choosing a suitable environment for such a ritual or ceremony. According to individuals like these, being in the right "frame of mind" is crucial for having a positive experience while under the influence of the hallucinogenic substance. This may be why individuals like Jean-Paul Sartre, who had a heavy and depressed mind, experienced hell after ingesting the cactus. This may also be why, in Native American Church ceremonies, those who take part have more consistent experiences due to possible mental and spiritual preparation that can or will most likely be dismissed by hard science. Peyote appears to be the most spiritual of all psychedelics apart from ayahuasca and should be treated with the necessary respect in order to avoid adverse consequences.

What Peyote Does to Your Mind and Body

After ingesting the substance, whether it be the dried or the mushy version, you can expect it to start working within 30 minutes to an hour after you've taken a bite or a swallow, whichever is the least detestable. Very much like ayahuasca, your initial experience will be unpleasant, and you will experience nausea, possible sweating and chills, and general discomfort. It is important to be aware that these symptoms can last for up to two hours. After the discomfort disappears, you will start to experience a feeling of complete numbness in your body. This sensation can be accompanied by other psychologically fuelled experiences, as well as some physical changes in your body. These include the following common symptoms:

- losing your appetite
- heightened senses
- dilated pupils
- an increase in your heart rate
- increased blood pressure levels
- synesthesia—when you experience seeing auditory things and hearing visual things
- a disconnection from reality
- hallucinations
- an impaired ability to control your limbs
- an increase in body temperature

There are also, as with all psychedelic substances, adverse effects that can occur if the substance is consumed without having the proper knowledge about it, and whether or not these effects are a possibility for you. Firstly, it is important to note that mescaline is not addictive; however, one does develop a tolerance, which means that larger doses would be required to get the same effects the more one uses the substance. This is also known as cross-tolerance, and it is actually common with most psychedelic drugs. To avoid experiencing cross-tolerance with mescaline, ensure that you only consume it, by the rule of thumb, about once a week. A user can also develop HPPD, or Hallucinogen Persisting Perception Disorder, which causes that nasty visual snow effect. Extreme cases of HPPD have also been recorded where prolonged episodes of hallucinations are prevalent. It is important to always know what you're doing or to have someone knowledgeable with you that can lead you during your trip.

Create The Best Setting for Your Own Peyote Ritual

If you want to take peyote or hold your own peyote healing ceremony, make sure you do it the right and safe way. Having an experienced guide with you is very important if you are not familiar with these types of ceremonies. If you don't have a professional guide at your disposal, you can also take someone along, usually referred to as a 'sitter,' who will remain sober throughout the process. The first and most important component that needs to be in the right place before you start a mescaline journey is your mindset. Start by thinking about why you are taking this substance and try to keep your thoughts pure and void of negativity. The setting or location where the ceremony is going to take place is also important for a safe and positive ceremony. It should be a setting where you feel safe and comfortable. Avoiding a noisy area is, for example, a good idea, as the noise can distract you and interfere with your experiences. Think more in terms of renting a cabin in the forest or in the mountains as the tranquility of nature around you will also inspire the process. If you want to heal yourself with a direct source from nature, the best place to do so is while being in the most natural setting you can find. If you are going with others and you enjoy making music, take instruments like drums and shakers to create a cozy and pleasant atmosphere. Remember that there is going to be a period where you're going to feel uncomfortable after ingesting the peyote.

Consider holding the ceremony at night-time, and make a fire as it is considered by the indigenous folks as a sacred element of the ceremony. If you feel that this is too close to appropriation, you can use another form of light like lanterns. Cleanse the ceremonial space with sage and use the words "so it is" during the cleansing process.

Remember practical details like dressing in comfortable and non-restrictive clothing as you will most likely be on a trip for at least eight hours. You can create your own inspirational invocations for your mescaline journey that support and manifest positivity in your mind to protect you throughout your journey (Seer, 2017).

Dried Peyote Dosage Guide:

- Light Dosage 3–6 small to medium buttons (10–20 grams)
- Typical Dosage 6–12 buttons (20–30 grams)
- Strong Dosage 8–16 buttons (30–40 grams)
- Heavy Dosage 15 or more buttons 40+ grams

Fresh Peyote Dosage Guide:

- Light Dosage 3–6 small to medium buttons (50–100 grams)

- Typical Dosage 6–12 buttons (100–150 grams)
- Strong Dosage 8–16 buttons (150–200 grams)
- Heavy Dosage 15 or more buttons 200+ grams (Seer, 2017).

When deciding to take peyote, a prudent way to start is by taking even less than a light dosage. The reason for this is, on the one hand, there are many who say that the effects of peyote are unpredictable and can cause unpleasant experiences; on the other hand, the advice is to prepare yourself and your environment, which will make your experience meaningful. Whichever way, starting small with a substance you've never taken before is always the smart way to go.

Dosage Guide

There are no set guidelines for microdosing with peyote; however, a recreational dose has been determined in terms of the level of mescaline in dried peyote buttons.

Recreational Dose	10 to 20 g of dried peyote buttons = 400 to 700 mg of mescaline

(Drugs.com, 2020)

Glossary of Terms

The glossary contains further information regarding scientific trials, their jargon, and key facts about the different scheduling phases of drugs as approved by the FDA. This information is for the reader's perusal and can be used to develop a deeper understanding of the context of different scientific clinical trials described in the book.

Addiction Research Center Inventory

A true/false questionnaire that was developed at the Addiction Research Center is used to assess the subjective effects of various drugs known to be abused. Components include statements such as:

- I have a nice feeling in my stomach.
- I am sweating more than I usually do.
- I feel like I'm floating.
- My bodily movements feel slower than normal.

The original version of this test had 550 of these statements, but newer and shorter versions have been developed and validated as well. The most widely used version of the test today includes only 49 items. Responses from the ARCI deliver scores on a variety of scales—five for the short form—that were empirically gathered by administering known drugs of abuse and putting in place the response pattern. For example, the Morphine-Benzedrine Group scale (MBG) is used as an agent for the euphoric effects produced by amphetamines and opioids (Scherrmann et al., 2010).

Breakthrough Therapy Designation

Breakthrough Therapy designation is a process specifically designed for the expedition of a drug's development, and reviewing said drug is designed to treat a serious condition. Furthermore, preliminary clinical evidence shows that the drug may testify to substantial improvement through available therapy on a clinically significant endpoint.

Determining whether the progress over available therapy is significant is a matter of judgment, and it depends on both the degree of the treatment's effect, which could include the duration of the effect and the significance of the observed clinical outcome. Generally, the preliminary clinical evidence should indicate a notable advantage over currently available therapy.

For the purposes of Breakthrough Therapy designation, "clinically significant endpoint" usually refers to measuring an effect on irreversible mortality or morbidity (IMM), or regards symptoms that show serious consequences of the disease in question. A clinically significant endpoint can also refer to specific findings suggesting an effect on serious symptoms, including:

- An effect on a settled surrogate endpoint.

- An effect on a surrogate endpoint or intermediate clinical endpoint that is considered reasonably likely to anticipate a clinical benefit—for example, the accelerated approval standard.
- An effect on pharmacodynamic biomarkers that doesn't meet any criteria for a suitable surrogate endpoint, but strongly suggests the potential for a clinically purposeful effect on the underlying disease.
- A notably improved safety profile compared to available therapy. For example, less dose-limiting toxicity for an oncology agent, with evidence of similar usefulness.
- A drug that receives Breakthrough Therapy designation qualifies for the following:
    1. Fast Track designation features
    2. Thorough guidance on an efficient drug development program, beginning as early as Phase 1
    3. Executive commitment involving senior managers

The drug company in question applies for the Breakthrough Therapy designation. If a sponsor has not applied for Breakthrough Therapy designation, the FDA can suggest that the sponsor consider submitting a request if:

(1) After reviewing submitted information and data—which includes preliminary clinical evidence—the Agency considers that the drug development program may meet the criteria for Breakthrough Therapy designation. Or,

(2) The outstanding drug development program can gain from the designation.

In an ideal setting, a Breakthrough Therapy designation application should be received by the FDA no later than the end of Phase II meetings if any of the features of the designation are to be obtained. Due to the primary intent of Breakthrough Therapy designation, which is developing evidence that is required to support approval as well-planned as possible, the FDA does not foresee that Breakthrough Therapy designation applications will be made after the submission of an original NDA, BLA, or a supplement. The FDA will respond to Breakthrough Therapy designation applications within sixty days of their reception of the request (Office of the Commissioner, 2018).

Constraint-Induced Movement Therapy

The term Constraint-Induced Movement Therapy (CIMT) sets out a collection of interventions that are designed to lower the impact of a stroke on the upper-limb (UL) function of some stroke survivors. CIMT is a behavioral approach to neuro-rehabilitation based on the concept of "learned non-use."

CIMT is mostly used for individuals following a cerebrovascular accident (CVA), as between 30–66% of CVA survivors will experience some degree of functional loss in their impaired limb(s). Furthermore, CIMT has also been used for individuals with traumatic brain injury (TBI), cerebral palsy (CP), and multiple sclerosis (MS). The goal of CIMT is to increase and improve the functionality of the more affected extremity while limiting the use of the less affected arm.

CIMT's three main elements include:

1. Structured, repetitive, practice-intensive therapy in the affected arm
2. Limiting the use of the less-affected arm
3. Applying a package of behavioral methods that transfer progress from the clinical setting to the real world—for example, increasing functionality.

The term CIMT comes from the studies of non-human primates in which somatosensory deafferentation of a single forelimb resulted in the animal ceasing use of the specific limb. Developed initially by Dr. Edward Taub, he showed that monkeys with surgical deafferentation of a forelimb stopped using the affected extremity. Through attempts, though failed, to use the deafferented forelimb, the monkeys started developing methods to compensate for their loss of an extremity. This newly learned behavior was eventually named "learned non-use."

Patients who have suffered a stroke need some hand function, a high level of motivation, a low level of cognitive dysfunction, and an adequate sense of balance and walking ability while wearing the restraint to be able to qualify for participation in these CIMT interventions.

The basic motor criterion for inclusion into therapy is:

- A 10° wrist extension
- A 10° finger extension
- A 10° thumb abduction

Clinical Intervention

1. Participants need to wear a mitt on the less-affected arm 90% of the time they are awake.

2. Participants need to perform repetitive task-oriented training with the affected arm for 6–7 hours per day.
3. These activities need to be performed for 10–15 consecutive weekdays.

There are three major components to these activities:

- Shaping is a method of training where a motor task is systematically made more difficult. Shaping programs are individualized to the patient's situation, consisting of 10–15 tasks that are selected basically from a primary battery of tasks. Each task is normally done in sets of 10–30 sec trials. At the end of each set of 10 trials, the task changes. However, only one shaping parameter will be altered at one time. This type of therapy requires constant involvement from a therapist.

- Task practice is the recurrent practice of individual and functional tasks that take 15–20mins. Rest is provided for the patient when they need it. Patients are frequently encouraged, and feedback is given at the end of every task to inform them about their performance. This activity does not require as much therapy involvement.

- A package of behavioral techniques is designed to transfer gains from the clinic to daily life. It includes a behavioral contract that identifies tasks that the participant will attempt to perform. Furthermore, this allows for the identification of barriers and problem solving to overcome these obstacles. The daily administration of the motor activity log promotes adherence (Physiopedia contributors, 2019).

Hallucinogen Rating Scale

The Hallucinogen Rating Scale (HRS) is a questionnaire widely used in the U.S. and Europe to evaluate the effects of several psychoactive substances, including hallucinogens. (Mizumoto et al., 2011)

Drug Enforcement Administration Mission Statement

> "*The mission of the Drug Enforcement Administration (DEA) is to enforce the controlled substances laws and regulations of the United States and bring to the criminal and civil justice system of the United States, or any other competent jurisdiction, those organizations and principal members of organizations, involved in the growing, manufacture, or distribution of controlled substances appearing in or destined for illicit traffic in the United States; and to recommend and support non-enforcement programs aimed at reducing the availability of illicit controlled substances on the domestic and international markets.*
>
> - *In carrying out its mission as the agency responsible for enforcing the controlled substances laws and regulations of the United States, the DEA's primary responsibilities include:*
>
> - *Investigation and preparation for the prosecution of major violators of controlled substance laws operating at interstate and international levels.*
>
> - *Investigation and preparation for prosecution of criminals and drug gangs who perpetrate violence in our communities and terrorize citizens through fear and intimidation.*

- *Management of a national drug intelligence program in cooperation with federal, state, local, and foreign officials to collect, analyze, and disseminate strategic and operational drug intelligence information.*

- *Seizure and forfeiture of assets derived from, traceable to, or intended to be used for illicit drug trafficking.*

- *Enforcement of the provisions of the Controlled Substances Act as they pertain to the manufacture, distribution, and dispensing of legally produced controlled substances.*

- *Coordination and cooperation with federal, state, and local law enforcement officials on mutual drug enforcement efforts and enhancement of such efforts through the exploitation of potential interstate and international investigations beyond local or limited federal jurisdictions and resources.*

- *Coordination and cooperation with federal, state, and local agencies, and with foreign governments, in programs designed to reduce the availability of illicit abuse-type drugs on the United States market through nonenforcement methods such as crop eradication, crop substitution, and training of foreign officials.*

- *Responsibility, under the policy guidance of the Secretary of State and U.S. Ambassadors, for all programs associated with drug law enforcement counterparts in foreign countries.*

- *Liaison with the United Nations, Interpol, and other organizations on matters relating to international drug control programs"* (United States Drug Enforcement Administration, 2019b).

Investigational New Drug Process

This is the process that needs to be followed in the United States if an application is to be submitted for approval regarding clinical trials.

The sponsor or drug developer needs to submit an Investigational New Drug (IND) application to the FDA before any clinical trials can begin for the testing of a new drug or substance.

IND Application

> The IND application has some compulsory requirements, which include
>
> 1. Clinical Protocols
> 2. Manufacturing information
> 3. Toxicity data and animal study data—this data must include any side-effects that may cause harm in human testing
> 4. Data from pre-existing human research, if any exists
> 5. Information about the investigator(s)

Applying for FDA Assistance

> When asking for FDA assistance, the research can go through the following phases, each following the former if it was deemed successful according to criteria.

1. Phase I

    Phase I remains a small study, and its purpose is to determine the safety of the drug and its dosage. The group of participants needs to be between 20 and 100 individuals, and they can either be chosen based on being generally healthy or because they suffer from a specific condition. The length of the Phase I study usually lasts a few months. After Phase I, approximately only 70% of tests move on to the next stage.

2. Phase II

    Phase II's purpose is to test the efficacy and possible side effects of the chemical compound used in the study. A Phase II study uses a slightly larger test group, which can be up to several hundred individuals who all have the relevant condition. A Phase II study can last from a few months to up to 2 years. After the completion of a Phase II protocol, only about 33% of studies are able to move to Phase III.

3. Phase III

    The focus of Phase III remains on efficacy and is also vigilant for any adverse effects any of the participants may experience during the trial. The length of a Phase III study is at least 1 year and can last up to 4 years, where between 300 and 3000 volunteers participate in the study. These participants all need to have the condition relevant to the testing. An average of 25–30%

of drugs qualifies for Phase VI testing after undergoing Phase III.

4. Phase IV

The final phase, which is Phase IV, is used to make sure there are no safety or efficacy concerns. In this phase, a few thousand participants who all suffer from the relevant condition are required to take part in the study.

FDA Approval

The FDA has up to 30 days to approve the original IND submission for a clinical trial. The purpose of this process is to offer protection to voluntary participants from any risks that may seem unreasonable or significant in the specific clinical trial. After the FDA receives an IND application or submission, it can respond in two ways:

1. It can approve the submission and trials can commence.
2. The FDA can decide on a clinical hold in order to stop or delay clinical trials. This decision needs to be based on one or more of the following reasons:
    - The investigators for the clinical trial are not qualified.
    - The materials presented to the volunteers or participants are in some way misleading.
    - The participants or volunteers are exposed to significant or unreasonable risk situations.
    - The IND application is not specific enough about the possible risks regarding the clinical trial.

FDA IND Review Team

In order to approve a clinical trial for any stage, there is a team of specialists, each looking at different aspects of the study and whether it was conducted properly and according to protocol.

- Project Manager

    The project manager is in charge of coordinating the team's role and activities during the review process. The project manager is also the primary contact person.

- Medical Officer

    The medical officer is involved throughout the entire trial process. It is their job to review all study information and clinical data from beginning to end.

- Statistician

    The statistician works with the medical officer, with the same data; however, their job is the evaluation of protocols and to look at the efficacy and safety of clinical research data.

- Chemist

    The chemist conducts an analysis on the drug in terms of how the drug was created, the stability of the drug, the focus on quality control, whether there are any impurities in the drug, and the potential continuity of the drug. This is all done by evaluating the chemical compounds of the drug.

- Pharmacologist

GLOSSARY OF TERMS

The job of the pharmacologist is to review existing preclinical studies for legitimacy purposes.

- Pharmakineticist

    The pharmakineticist needs to look at several aspects of the drug's performance. These include how the drug is metabolized, the absorption potential, the distribution of the drug after administration, and the relevant excretion processes regarding relevant hormones. They are also in charge of interpreting the blood-level data using a time-interval approach, which assists them in the assessment of a suitable dosage and how the drug needs to be administered.

- Microbiologist

    The microbiologist is in charge of reviewing the submitted data and focuses on the assessment of microbial responses if the drug being tested is an antimicrobial drug (Office of the Commissioner, 2019).

MAOI

MAOI stands for monoamine oxidase inhibitor. MAOIs inhibit the breakdown of neurotransmitters like serotonin, dopamine, and noradrenaline, which increases the concentration of the neurotransmitter in the brain. They also include well-known antidepressant medication.

Pharmacodynamics

Pharmacodynamics, described as what a drug does to the body, or a drug's effects on the body, is the study of the molecular, biochemical, and physiologic effects of drugs on the body. It involves processes like receptor binding, which includes receptor sensitivity, post-receptor effects, and chemical interactions. Pharmacodynamics, with pharmacokinetics (what the body does to a drug), helps explain the relationship between the dose and response, or the drug's effects. The pharmacologic response depends on the drug's ability to bind to its target. The concentration of the drug at the receptor site influences the drug's effect.

A drug's pharmacodynamics can be affected by physiological changes in an individual:

- Aging process
- A disorder or disease
- Other drugs

Disorders that can affect pharmacodynamic responses in the body include malnutrition, genetic mutations, thyrotoxicosis, and myasthenia gravis. Also included are Parkinson's disease, some forms of insulin resistance, and diabetes mellitus (type-2 diabetes). These disorders can alter receptor binding, change the level of binding proteins, and lower receptor sensitivity. Aging tends to affect pharmacodynamic responses through post-receptor response sensitivity and alterations in receptor binding (Abimbola, 2019).

Pharmacokinetics

Pharmacokinetics, also described as "what the body does to a drug," refers to the journey of a drug into, through, and out of the body, including the course of time of its absorption, bioavailability, distribution, metabolism, and excretion.

Pharmacodynamics involves chemical interactions, receptor binding, and post-receptor effects. Drug pharmacokinetics determines the onset, intensity, and duration of a drug's effect on the human body. Formulas relating to the above-mentioned processes summarize the pharmacokinetic behavior of most medications. The pharmacokinetics of a drug depends on the drug's chemical properties and patient-related factors. Some patient-related factors like the function of the kidneys, an individual's genetic makeup, age, and sex can be used to predict the pharmacokinetic parameters in different populations. For example, the half-life of certain medications, especially those that require both physiological metabolism and excretion, may be extraordinarily long in older people. Additionally, physiological changes that come with aging affect many aspects of pharmacokinetics.

Other factors are related to an individual's physiology. The effects of some individual factors, for example, kidney failure, dehydration, obesity, and hepatic failure can be predicted reasonably, but other factors are idiosyncratic and are thus unpredictable in terms of effects. Due to individual differences, drug administration must be based on each patient's individual needs. These needs are determined traditionally, by empirically adjusting dosage until the therapeutic goal is achieved. This approach, however, is often lacking because it can delay the required response or it can result in adverse effects.

Knowledge of pharmacokinetic principles helps prescribers like doctors adjust dosage more accurately and rapidly. The application of pharmacokinetic principles with the aim to individualize pharmacotherapy is called therapeutic drug monitoring (LE, 2018).

Pharmacology

Pharmacology is the science of drugs and their effect on living systems. You will be able to find pharmacology present all around you. In your medicine cabinet at home, when you visit your doctor or the dentist, and when you visit the chemist. Pharmacology is responsible for the development of painkillers, caffeine drinks, and antibiotics, to give a few examples. It is the science of the process in your body when it interacts with a given drug. Every medication we take alters the chemistry within our bodies in a certain way. The role of pharmacology is to understand why and how these changes take place, which then allows the more effective medication to be developed.

Pharmacology is crucial for:

- Discovering new medications to help fight illness.
- The improvement of the effectiveness of medicines.
- The reduction of negative or unwanted side effects of medication
- Aiming to understand why individuals respond differently to certain drugs.

Pharmacology lies at the center of biomedical science, and it links chemistry, pathology, and physiology. Pharmacologists work closely with a wide variety of other scientific fields that make up modern biomedical science, including immunology, cancer biology, neuroscience, and molecular and cellular biology.

Pharmacological knowledge and research improves the lives of millions of people across the world. It maximizes their benefit and minimizes risk and harm.

As new diseases develop, and older medicines no longer work as efficiently, the contribution of pharmacology to finding more efficient and safer medication becomes all the more important (British Pharmacological Society, 2019).

United States Scheduling Procedures and Guidelines

Pharmaceutical drugs, specific chemicals, and other substances that can be used to make drugs are classified into five categories called 'Schedules.' The level the substance is placed under depends on whether the drug has an acceptable medical function and whether the drug has a high or low potential for abuse by the user. A drug that has a high potential for abuse is also most likely a drug that will form a relationship of dependence with the user. The dependence referred to here can both be physiological or psychological. Schedule I drugs represent drugs that pose the highest danger for abuse, and Schedule V drugs represent those that pose the lowest abuse-related risk. The Controlled Substance Act contains a list of drugs categorized according to their scheduling in alphabetical order. Here are the basic requirements of all the drug schedules.

- Schedule I Drugs

    Schedule I drugs are classified as drugs that have no known medical use or purpose, according to the DEA, and also have a very high potential for abuse. Examples of these drugs include *methaqualone*, *heroin*, *LSD*, and *peyote*.

- Schedule II Drugs

    Schedule II drugs are also defined as drugs that have a high potential for abuse by the user and that can potentially cause serious physiological or psychological dependence. Additionally, Schedule II drugs are considered to be dangerous. Examples of Schedule II drugs are cocaine, methadone, Vicodin, methamphetamine, Ritalin or Adderall, Hydromorphone, fentanyl, oxycodone or OxyContin, and meperidine or Demerol.

- Schedule III Drugs

    Schedule III drugs can be chemicals or substances that are defined as drugs with a moderate-to-low potential for psychological and physical dependence. Schedule III drugs' abuse potential is lower than Schedule I and II drugs but remains higher than Schedule IV drugs. Here are some examples of Schedule III drugs: Products that contain less than 90 mg of codeine per dosage unit, for example, Tylenol with codeine, anabolic steroids, ketamine, and testosterone

- Schedule IV Drugs

    Schedule IV drugs, chemicals, or substances, can be defined as drugs with a decreased potential of dependence and also a

Glossary of Terms

decreased risk for abuse. Some examples of Schedule IV drugs include Xanax, Valium, Ativan, Tramadol, Ambien, Soma, Darvon, Darvocet, Talwin.

- Schedule V Drugs

Finally, Schedule V drugs are chemicals, or substances, that are defined as drugs with a much lower potential for abuse than Schedule IV, and these drugs consist of preparations that contain limited quantities of specific narcotics. Schedule V drugs are generally used for analgesic, antidiarrheal, and antitussive purposes. Some examples of Schedule V drugs include Cough preparations that contain less than 200 milligrams of codeine or per 100 milliliters (Robitussin AC), Motofen, Lyrica, Lomotil, and Parepectolin (United States Drug Enforcement Administration, 2019a).

Visual Analog Scale

The Visual Analog Scale (VAS) is a measurement instrument that strives in measuring characteristics or attitudes that, in a particular context, are understood to be cataloged across perennial values and thus cannot be measured directly at the highest level of efficiency. The Visual Analog Scale is often used for clinical research purposes to measure aspects like the intensity or frequency of different symptoms specific to the research (Physiopedia contributors, 2021).

For example, the amount of pleasure or pain that a patient might be experiencing will range across a continuum, from no pain or pleasure to extreme pain or pleasure. From the patient's perspective, this "pleasure or pain" spectrum comes across as continuous. Their pain levels do not make individual or distinct leaps, as with the usual categorization of none, mild, moderate, and severe would suggest. Therefore, the VAS scale was created to capture the concept of an underlying continuum. So, the main purpose of the VAS is to provide a unidimensional method of measuring an abstract experience such as pleasure or pain and its intensity. A VAS can manifest in more than one structure, which includes:

- scales with a middle point and graduations or numbers like numerical rating scales
- meter-shaped scales like curvilinear analog scales
- "box-scales" consisting of circles placed at equal distances from each other
- scales with descriptive terms at intervals similar to a line like Likert scales or graphic rating scales

The most simple VAS is a straight, horizontal, fixed-length line that is, in most cases, 100mm long. Both ends are defined as the extreme limits for measuring symptoms like pain or other health-related symptoms. The scale is orientated from the left, which indicates the worst, and to the right, which indicates the best. In several studies, horizontal scales are orientated from right to left, but many other researchers prefer to use vertical VAS scales. The scales are normally completed by patients or the individual suffering from the symptoms themselves, but it is sometimes also used to evoke opinions from health professionals.

The patient will mark on the line the point that they feel represents their perception of their current experience of the symptom in question. The VAS score is then calculated by measuring in millimeters from the left-hand end of the line to the point that the patient marks. If the scale works from the other side, or if the scale is vertical, the calculation would be done accordingly (Physiopedia contributors, 2021).

Conclusion

The Psychedelic Renaissance in Full Swing

The first probes into these psychedelic substances in the earlier part of the twentieth century were naive as researchers started their experiments with a lack of understanding of what they were working with. However, they managed to give us a glimpse of how beneficial these substances can be for our mental health and wellbeing before their frantic banning in the '70s was put in place by multiple governments and their various regulations by global institutions. In the past two decades, research has emerged again, becoming ever more bold and prominent. Leading institutions we can thank for the growth of the Psychedelic Renaissance include John Hopkins University, UCLA, and NYU. Other independent institutions include ARUPA and MAPS.

The renaissance is about rediscovering and redefining these substances, educating the public and the healthcare industry, and creating a platform so convincing that their legalization should be undeniable. Here is a recap of what we know so far about each substance's potential:

MDMA

Prominent figures that used MDMA as a therapeutic tool are also known for developing a specific methodology they would use when administering patients with MDMA during treatment. Leo Zeff, for example, is known for setting ground rules before a session and playing music while each participant is given glasses to place over their eyes. Some of these methods were adopted by other therapists too, like Ann Shulgin. Current research shows that MDMA shows promising potential for the treatment of depression and PTSD. These trials are still in their preliminary stages; however, their results have made researchers confident that they will be granted permission to continue with their work. MDMA has come a long way from being just known as a street drug.

Magic Mushrooms

The history and timeline of psilocybin's use is still a hot debate among botanists and archaeologists. This curious fungus was used in Timothy Leary's famous Concord Prison Experiment before he started using psychedelic drugs for spiritual and political purposes. Researchers today think that this experiment is worthy of reviewing and that the reason it failed is because of a minor lack of planning from Leary and his team. The fact that researchers see potential in Leary's thought process back then is a prima facie indication that psilocybin has therapeutic potential. Interestingly enough, this mushroom is not fully banned in all countries; for example, in Samoa, it is completely legal, and in Canada, it is legal for therapeutic use, which is a huge forward leap for researchers in this field. The legalization in Canada is predominantly thanks to a relatively new and popular practice applied to a few psychedelics, but specifically magic mushrooms—microdosing. This has produced positive feedback in spades for psilocybin. Instead of taking a recreational dose of psilocybin, only a sliver is taken, so those who consume it don't need to worry about hallucinating. Even better, is said to make an individual more 'mindful.' Finally, psilocybin has also been used in research on major depression with positive results.

LSD

LSD can be traced all the way back to the Salem Witch trials if historians' accounts are to be believed. One of the main components of LSD is ergot, which grows on grains in damp conditions, and if consumed, especially in large quantities, can cause hallucinations, and conclusions. The reemergence of LSD, though, showed the opposite effect of its fungal parent, and it has a promising repertoire of therapeutic uses where other psychedelics do not. It has, for example, shown promising effects when it comes to the treatment of Autism Spectrum Disorder when combined with MDMA in order to balance out the experience. Though its history becomes clouded with suspicion mid-century, the ground-breaking study which uncovered LSD's ability to separate the human consciousness from the actual neurological functioning of the brain cannot be ignored. LSD is a force to be reckoned with.

DMT

The famous Spirit Molecule is a curious one because of its presence in our own bodies, especially in the brain. DMT is also present in certain plants that ancient civilizations used to make a brew with, causing them to have otherworldly experiences. DMT is known for its intense trips, and some researchers hypothesize that our brain, or more specifically the pineal gland in the brain, secretes a large amount of DMT before we die or when we have a near-death experience. If you don't want to take a recreational dose and experience visions of elves, DMT can also be used successfully as a form of treatment for depression. It has been a subject of clinical research, and it has proven to be a very effective treatment for substance abuse and addictive disorders. It is curious to think that this powerful substance comes from within us and when we reinsert it, it can have these incredible healing effects.

Ayahuasca

Ayahuasca is closely related to DMT, as we now know that it is a brew that has been concocted for thousands of years by indigenous tribes in the Amazon and that one of its ingredients is a plant containing DMT. The genius behind this brew is that this plant, which contains MAOIs, causes the DMT to stay active when taken orally—archeologists and botanists cannot understand how the isolated Amazonians have the knowledge of this; they posit that it is also an unlikely coincidence. Ayahuasca is legal for spiritual and ceremonial use, and many are interested in its mental healing effects. However, going through the whole ayahuasca journey is not always a pleasant experience. Its cleansing phase, or purga, gets rid of all toxins in your body before the hallucinations begin. If you ever plan to ingest ayahuasca, always let a shaman guide you through the process.

Peyote

Peyote, the interesting little blue-green cactus with the buttons will have you tripping on the alkaloid it contains that is known as mescaline. This plant only grows in parts of Mexico and Southwestern parts of North America and is used by indigenous peoples for ritualistic purposes. Peyote is also known for its antibiotic effect and is used by the indigenous peoples to clean wounds and cuts on their bodies, as well as soothe insect bite marks. It cost the Native American Church a legal battle to gain the right to use this sacred plant as part of their rituals and ceremonies, and its use also spread to Canada as many Native Americans were forced over the border in the northern United States.

It is crucial that not only researchers, but also healthcare practitioners and the public, keep an open mind about these substances as most of these groups currently, and have for several generations, perceive them as stigmatized, dangerous, and illegal drugs. It is quite interesting to look back at how these substances reached their ultimate high in research potential, and then their ultimate low in the classification of Schedule I substances, in the span of fifty years. If they had so much potential then, the sudden downward spiral and bad publicity for substances like psilocybin could not have been a natural or spontaneous state of affairs.

For a long time, the only place psychedelics could be found was at music festivals, when they could have helped millions improve their lives if they were optionally available as treatment options at clinics. Even more, some substances have shown healing potential that stretches further than only treating psychological conditions. The way we view psychedelics today is due to a combined effort from the media, government, and society to some degree as just a bit more than a half-century ago, scientists were genuinely excited about the potential of psilocybin, LSD, MDMA, and DMT. It is possible that the antics of Timothy Leary and his transformation of the use of these substances could have been the catalyst for change.

As we've shown in this book, there have been some astounding discoveries through preliminary research that can turn healthcare—specifically mental healthcare—on its head. This, of course, implies that the pharmaceutical industry as we know it will also be turned on its head and that Big Pharma and all of its stakeholders may lose their monopoly over the healthcare industry. How will they respond?

This is our status quo on psychedelics and their potential. Something tells us that there is much more to come, but as the famous quantum physicist and Nobel Laureate, Max Planck, said, "science evolves one funeral at a time" (Bell, 2017).

References

Abbott, A. (2019). Altered minds: mescaline's complicated history. *Nature, 569*(7757), 485–486. https://doi.org/10.1038/d41586-019-01571-2

Abimbola, F. (2019, June). *Overview of pharmacodynamics*. MSD Manual Professional Edition; MSD Manuals. https://www.msdmanuals.com/professional/clinical-pharmacology/pharmacodynamics/overview-of-pharmacodynamics

Abo, S. (2020). *Revolutionary drug trial could see ecstasy used as prescription medicine for those living with PTSD and mental illness*. 9now.nine.com.au. https://9now.nine.com.au/60-minutes/revolutionary-mdma-trial-changing-lives-of-those-with-mental-illness-60-minutes/6e9f2a9d-e88c-49b5-9654-a2636fec7db9

Alcohol and Drug Foundation. (2018, July 19). *LSD as a therapeutic treatment - Alcohol and Drug Foundation*. Adf.org.au. https://adf.org.au/insights/lsd-therapeutic-treatment/

Algernon Pharmaceuticals. (2021, February 1). *Algernon Pharmaceuticals launches stroke treatment clinical research program with psychedelic drug DMT "The Spirit Molecule."* GlobeNewswire News Room. https://www.globenewswire.com/news-release/2021/02/01/2167200/0/en/

Algernon-Pharmaceuticals-Launches-Stroke-Treatment-Clinical-Research-Program-with-Psychedelic-Drug-DMT-The-Spirit-Molecule.html

Beckley Foundation. (2017, July 14). *Ayahuasca stimulates the birth of new brain cells*. The Beckley Foundation. https://www.beckleyfoundation.org/ayahuasca-stimulates-the-birth-of-new-brain-cells/

Begley, S. (2018, August 23). *"Microdosing" is touted by 'shroomers and Reddit users. Science is starting to test their claims — and finding some truth.* STAT; STAT. https://www.statnews.com/2018/08/23/science-testing-claimed-benefits-of-psilocybin-microdosing/

Bell, B. (2017, October 9). *The psychedelic renaissance is here. Will it last this time?* Massive Science. https://massivesci.com/articles/psychedelic-research-renaissance-culture/

Bouso, J. C., & Riba, J. (2014, November). *Ayahuasca and the treatment of drug addiction*. ResearchGate; Springer. https://www.researchgate.net/publication/330967162_Ayahuasca_and_the_Treatment_of_Drug_Addiction

Britannica. (2021). *Indole | chemical compound*. Encyclopedia Britannica. https://www.britannica.com/science/indole

British Pharmacological Society. (2019). *What is pharmacology?* Bps.ac.uk. https://www.bps.ac.uk/about/about-pharmacology/what-is-pharmacology

Carhart-Harris, R. L., & Goodwin, G. M. (2017). The therapeutic potential of psychedelic drugs: Past, present, and future. *Neuropsychopharmacology, 42*(11), 2105–2113. https://doi.org/10.1038/npp.2017.84

Carhart-Harris, R. L., Roseman, L., Bolstridge, M., Demetriou, L., Pannekoek, J. N., Wall, M. B., Tanner, M., Kaelen, M., McGonigle, J., Murphy, K., Leech, R., Curran, H. V., & Nutt, D. J. (2017). Psilocybin for treatment-resistant depression: MRI-measured brain mechanisms. *Scientific Reports*, *7*(1). https://doi.org/10.1038/s41598-017-13282-7

Centro Espírita Beneficente Uniao Do Vegetal. (2020). *UDV Supreme Court case*. Centro Espírita Beneficente União Do Vegetal in the United States. https://udvusa.org/supreme-court-case

Corbetta, D., Sirtori, V., Castellini, G., Moja, L., & Gatti, R. (2016). Constraint-induced movement therapy for upper extremities in people with stroke. *Stroke*, *47*(8). https://doi.org/10.1161/strokeaha.116.013281

Davis, K. (2017, March 24). *DMT: Side effects, facts, and health risks*. Www.medicalnewstoday.com. https://www.medicalnewstoday.com/articles/306889#facts

Deeth, S. (2020, June 4). *New trial ordered for thomas chan*. Global News. https://globalnews.ca/news/7024786/new-trial-ordered-thomas-chan/#:~:text=Andrew%20Chan%2C%20and%20attack%20on

Deutsche Welle. (2006, August 18). *Merck digs up truth about role in the birth of ecstasy | DW | 18.08.2006*. DW.COM. https://www.dw.com/en/merck-digs-up-truth-about-role-in-the-birth-of-ecstasy/a-2140190

DiPaolo, M. (2018). *LSD and the hippies: A focused analysis of criminalization and persecution in the sixties | the people, ideas, and things (PIT) Journal*. Unc.edu. http://pitjournal.unc.edu/content/lsd-and-hippies-focused-analysis-criminalization-and-persecution-sixties

Dishotsky, N. I., Loughman, W. D., Mogar, R. E., & Lipscomb, W. R. (1971). LSD and genetic damage. *Science (New York, N.Y.), 172*(3982), 431–440. https://doi.org/10.1126/science.172.3982.431

Doblin, R. (1998). Dr. Leary's concord prison experiment: A 34-year follow-up study. *Journal of Psychoactive Drugs, 30*(4), 419–426. https://doi.org/10.1080/02791072.1998.10399715

Dolan, E. W. (2021, January 30). *Neuroscience study indicates that LSD "frees" brain activity from anatomical constraints.* PsyPost. https://www.psypost.org/2021/01/neuroscience-study-indicates-that-lsd-frees-brain-activity-from-anatomical-constraints-59458

Drugs.com. (2014, May 18). *LSD.* Drugs.com; Drugs.com. https://www.drugs.com/illicit/lsd.html

Drugs.com. (2020, July 22). *Peyote uses, benefits & dosage - drugs.com herbal database.* Drugs.com. https://www.drugs.com/npp/peyote.html

Drugs.com. (2021). *Psilocybin (magic mushrooms) uses, effects & hazards.* Drugs.com. https://www.drugs.com/illicit/psilocybin.html#legal-status

Dunne, C. (2018, December 6). Welcome to the trip of your life: The rise of underground LSD guides. *The Guardian.* https://www.theguardian.com/society/2018/dec/06/lsd-guides-psychedelic-assisted-psychotherapy

Dyck, E. (2017). *A psychedelic renaissance: Historical reflections on the future.* MAPS. https://maps.org/news/bulletin/articles/420-bulletin-spring-2017/6620-a-psychedelic-renaissance-historical-reflections-on-the-future

Dyck, E., & Bradford, T. (2012). Peyote on the prairies: Religion, scientists, and native-newcomer relations in Western Canada. *Journal of Canadian Studies*, *46*(1), 28–52. https://doi.org/10.3138/jcs.46.1.28

Eskin, T. (2021, January 28). *Why isn't Big Pharma jumping into psychedelics?* PsyTech. https://psytechglobal.com/big-pharma-psychedelics/

Fairmount Behavioral Health System. (2021). *Hallucinogens and Schizophrenia*. https://fairmountbhs.com/patients-families/resources/hallucinogens-and-schizophrenia/?__cf_chl_captcha_tk__=c4f6c5987796ce90540129e11bf94d7fcd8fa1d6-1616392967-0-AReUEwezPShOUVip6gxwSCWm-c3xDzkkiWo19CKTHxmDGmGZYW0Ebh-Tvp62dEqwot-NZ1L_iybTgoXp4b-rJPgoWH-QKHM3smtne64Tqvq1cr4Nt54Q6wpm9prIcd6jZ0EYnk_4k0M51IVyDIv-_PeBK2WB5GOhVRgPD-lTgthHRotyEG548fHbhDWTZUMX9wLErimsg4_5kMc8Z1TsaAHSUC5q19TkTYuXe0keW74Rqe3sb9jtUSZBU-Fvse0rjSS4uxR2IXvgwjyWdq7Q8uHV6lwWc1oeAMFXw0-7dlkMYU3c2DQo5GBHsPPtUJ0eJ9vhjK9NJy-Kp8zk8JLm8npZ6mOW8bVpMyx66jHSVKChjQowBblmdw0GuVCaJExLD5W8ZOacBjRn-6iS5PWp37h-Ey8yf8h2CUR6PR8Xn33v35DDWRHX1tNaNmxeDjLIfKVMSE1tI0dWXRkYMmxfYW9Lhd_2Qr7_WSsPoU0UrXvha27PXiTsqCqgBfbg0FM_8b_qjIFl_7n-rVMnIxjZ4I90MymRKYu8IMQ1UA1dRmVDN4Q45rJUuU29dGfUStXXmXurUPh502JcPTHGN6eDFpeMVSH8XdLLHnz-mNCVnn2h

Freeman, S., & Chandler, N. (2009, February 25). *How magic mushrooms work*. HowStuffWorks. https://science.howstuffworks.com/magic-mushroom6.htm

Fuentes, J. J., Fonseca, F., Elices, M., Farré, M., & Torrens, M. (2020). Therapeutic use of LSD in psychiatry: A systematic review of randomized-controlled clinical trials. *Frontiers in Psychiatry, 10.* https://doi.org/10.3389/fpsyt.2019.00943

Geddes, L. (2020, December 9). *Psychedelic drug DMT to be trialled in UK to treat depression.* The Guardian. https://www.theguardian.com/science/2020/dec/09/psychedelic-drug-dmt-to-be-trialled-in-uk-to-treat-depression

Gustin, D. B. (2020, May 26). *MDMA microdosing for depression and anxiety | Dr. Gustin's blog.* Toxicologyexpert.net. https://toxicologyexpert.net/dr.-gustin-s-blog/mdma-microdosing-for-depression-and-anxiety.html

Haridy, R. (2020, August 26). *Landmark clinical trial exploring LSD-MDMA combo to begin late 2020.* New Atlas. https://newatlas.com/science/landmark-clinical-trial-lsd-mdma-mindmed/

Hartney, E. (2012, February 26). *What to know about magic mushroom use.* Verywell Mind; Verywell Mind. https://www.verywellmind.com/what-are-magic-mushrooms-22085

History.com Editors. (2018, August 21). *LSD.* HISTORY. https://www.history.com/topics/crime/history-of-lsd

History.com Editors. (2021). *MDMA.* HISTORY. https://www.history.com/topics/crime/history-of-mdma#section_2

ICEERS. (2019, January 25). *Treading carefully in unpredictable times: Recent legal incidents in the USA.* ICEERS. https://www.iceers.org/treading-carefully-in-unpredictable-times-recent-legal-incidents-in-the-usa/

References

Jefferson, R. S. (2019, September 12). *Magic mushrooms as medicine? Johns Hopkins scientists launch center for psychedelic research. say psychedelics could treat Alzheimer's, depression and addiction.* Forbes. https://www.forbes.com/sites/robinseatonjefferson/2019/09/12/magic-mushrooms-as-medicine-johns-hopkins-scientists-launch-center-for-psychedelic-research-say-psychedelics-could-treat-alzheimers-depression-and-addiction/?sh=2190cc11c171

Kenney, A. (2019, August 23). *Spores of a psychedelic mushroom industry are sprouting in Denver after decriminalization.* The Denver Post; The Denver Post. https://www.denverpost.com/2019/08/23/psychedelic-mushrooms-denver-decriminalization/

Kitchens, S. (2018, May 3). *Everything you need to know about microdosing's micromoment.* The Cut. https://www.thecut.com/2018/05/microdosing-guide-and-explainer.html

Krupic, J. (2017). Wire together, fire apart. *Science, 357*(6355), 974–975. https://doi.org/10.1126/science.aao4159

Kubala, J. (2019, June 26). *What is ayahuasca? Experience, benefits, and side effects.* Healthline; Healthline Media. https://www.healthline.com/nutrition/ayahuasca#uses

LE, J. (2018). *Overview of pharmacokinetics.* MSD Manual Professional Edition; MSD Manuals. https://www.msdmanuals.com/professional/clinical-pharmacology/pharmacokinetics/overview-of-pharmacokinetics

Lohnes, K. (2019). How rye bread may have caused the Salem witch trials. In *Encyclopædia Britannica.* https://www.britannica.com/story/how-rye-bread-may-have-caused-the-salem-witch-trials

Lynch, M. (2019, August 19). *"Magic mushroom" drug receives breakthrough therapy designation.* Outsourcing-Pharma.com. https://www.outsourcing-pharma.com/Article/2018/10/26/Magic-mushroom-drug-receives-breakthrough-therapy-designation

MacKenzie, R. J. (2020, December 10). *World-First clinical trial explores safety and efficacy of DMT for Major Depression.* Neuroscience from Technology Networks. https://www.technologynetworks.com/neuroscience/news/world-first-clinical-trial-explores-safety-and-efficacy-of-dmt-for-major-depression-343822

MacKenzie, R. J. (2021, January 5). *New clinical trial explores safety of DMT for substance use disorders.* Neuroscience from Technology Networks. https://www.technologynetworks.com/neuroscience/blog/new-clinical-trial-explores-safety-of-dmt-for-substance-use-disorders-344262

Mammoser, G. (2017, May 1). *Microdosing: Benefits and risks.* Healthline. https://www.healthline.com/health-news/the-benefits-risks-with-microdosing#Author

Mammoser, G. (2019a, February 12). *Mushrooms as medicine? Psychedelics may be next breakthrough treatment.* Healthline; Healthline Media. https://www.healthline.com/health-news/benefits-of-medical-mushrooms#The-state-of-psilocybin-research-

Mammoser, G. (2019b, December 1). *What happens to the brain after taking the hallucinogenic in ayahuasca.* Healthline. https://www.healthline.com/health-news/what-happens-to-your-brain-on-ayahuasca#What-the-study-found

MAPS. (2017). *Phase 3 program: MDMA-Assisted psychotherapy for PTSD - MAPS.* MAPS. https://maps.org/research/mdma/ptsd/phase3

Martin, A. (2021, January 27). *LSD breakthrough could enable treatment for autism and social anxiety, research finds.* Sky News. https://news.sky.com/story/lsd-breakthrough-could-enable-treatment-for-autism-and-social-anxiety-research-finds-12200193

Mizumoto, S., Silveira, D. X. da, Barbosa, P. C. R. & Strassman, R. J. (2011). Hallucinogen Rating Scale (HRS) - Versão brasileira: tradução e adaptação transcultural. *Archives of Clinical Psychiatry (São Paulo), 38*(6), 231–237. https://doi.org/10.1590/s0101-60832011000600004

News 18. (2020, November 19). *Canada makes consumption of psychedelic mushrooms legal for people with depression.* News18. https://www.news18.com/news/buzz/canada-makes-consumption-of-psychedelic-mushrooms-legal-for-people-with-depression-3096260.html

Nofil, B. (2019). *The CIA's appalling human experiments with mind control.* HISTORY. https://www.history.com/mkultra-operation-midnight-climax-cia-lsd-experiments

Office of the Commissioner. (2018). *Breakthrough therapy designation.* U.S. Food and Drug Administration. https://www.fda.gov/patients/fast-track-breakthrough-therapy-accelerated-approval-priority-review/breakthrough-therapy

Office of the Commissioner. (2019). *Step 3: Clinical research.* U.S. Food and Drug Administration. https://www.fda.gov/patients/drug-development-process/step-3-clinical-research

Palmer, J. (2016, December 5). *Why is DMT illegal?* Julian Palmer. http://julianpalmerism.com/why-is-dmt-illegal/

Passie, T. (2018). The early use of MDMA ("ecstasy") in psychotherapy (1977–1985). *Drug Science, Policy and Law, 4*(10), 205032451876744. https://doi.org/10.1177/2050324518767442

Physiopedia contributors. (2019, September 13). *Constraint induced movement therapy*. Physiopedia. https://www.physio-pedia.com/Constraint_Induced_Movement_Therapy

Physiopedia contributors. (2021, February 22). *Visual analogue scale*. Physiopedia; Physiopedia. https://www.physio-pedia.com/Visual_Analogue_Scale#:~:text=A%20Visual%20Analogue%20Scale%20

PsychonautWiki. (2021). Ayahuasca brew. PsychonautWiki. https://psychonautwiki.org/wiki/Ayahuasca_brew#Ingredients

Reality Sandwich. (2019a, July 17). *DMT substance guide: Effects, common uses, safety*. Realitysandwich.com. https://realitysandwich.com/dmt-guide/

Reality Sandwich. (2019b, July 17). *MDMA & ecstasy guide: Effects, common uses, safety*. Realitysandwich.com. https://realitysandwich.com/mdma-guide/

Reality Sandwich. (2019c, October 4). *Peyote guide: Effects, common uses, safety*. Realitysandwich.com. https://realitysandwich.com/ultimate-peyote-guide-effects-common-uses-safety/

Reality Sandwich. (2019d, December 5). *Ayahuasca guide: Effects, common uses, safety*. Realitysandwich.com. https://realitysandwich.com/ayahuasca-guide/

Richtert, L. (2019, August 4). *The psychedelic renaissance*. Psychology Today. https://www.psychologytoday.com/za/blog/hygieias-workshop/201908/the-psychedelic-renaissance

Roberts, G. D. (2014, April 2). *Blasting off with Dr. DMT*. Www.vice.com. https://www.vice.com/en/article/bn5je3/blasting-off-with-dr-dmt

Santos-Longhurst, A., & Carter, A. (2019, November 19). *What is DMT? Everything you need to know.* Healthline. https://www.healthline.com/health/what-is-dmt

Scherrmann, J.-M., Wolff, K., Franco, C. A., Potenza, M. N., Uzbay, T., Bizarro, L., Roberts, D. C. S., Balster, R. L., Walsh, S. L., Mason, B. J., Heyser, C. J., Riley, A. L., Kohut, S., Wadenberg, M.-L. G., Wilkins, H., Newhouse, P., Jackson, A., Uys, J. D., Kalivas, P. W., & Harvey, V. L. (2010). Addiction Research Center Inventory. *Encyclopedia of Psychopharmacology*, 20–20. https://doi.org/10.1007/978-3-540-68706-1_938

Seer, B. (2017, September 28). *The beginner's guide to healing with peyote*. EntheoNation. https://entheonation.com/blog/beginners-guide-healing-peyote/

Sheikh, K. (2016, November 30). *MDMA could be on the market legally by 2021*. Popular Science. https://www.popsci.com/fda-just-approved-final-stage-mdma-drug-trials/

Siebert, A. (2020, November 13). *Microdosing psychedelics is trendy, but does it work? Here's what science says.* Forbes. https://www.forbes.com/sites/amandasiebert/2020/11/13/microdosing-psychedelics-is-trendy-but-does-it-work-heres-what-science-says/?sh=2621afaacf7c

Sissons, B. (2020, May 19). *Is MDMA a viable depression treatment? Research and more*. Www.medicalnewstoday.com. https://www.medicalnewstoday.com/articles/mdma-depression#mdma-and-depression

Solomon, A. (2011, May 3). *Interview: Dr. Rick Strassman*. Boing Boing. https://boingboing.net/2011/05/03/strassman.html

Strassman, R. (2001). DMT: the spirit molecule; a doctor's revolutionary research into the biology of near-death and mystical experiences. In *Internet Archive*. Rochester, Vt. : Park Street Press. https://archive.org/details/dmtspiritmolecul00rick

Strassman, R. J. (1994). Dose-Response study of N,N-Dimethyltryptamine in humans. *Archives of General Psychiatry, 51*(2), 98. https://doi.org/10.1001/archpsyc.1994.03950020022002

Strassman, R. J., Peake, G. T., Qualls, C. R., & Lisansky, E. J. (1987). A model for the study of the acute effects of melatonin in man. *The Journal of Clinical Endocrinology & Metabolism, 65*(5), 847–852. https://doi.org/10.1210/jcem-65-5-847

Szára, S. (1994). Are hallucinogens psychoheuristic? *NIDA Research Monograph, 146*, 33–51. PubMed.

The American Presidency Project. (1978, August 12). *American Indian Religious Freedom Statement on Signing S.J. Res. 102 Into Law. | The American Presidency Project*. Www.presidency.ucsb.edu. https://www.presidency.ucsb.edu/documents/american-indian-religious-freedom-statement-signing-sj-res-102-into-law

The Editors of Encyclopaedia Britannica. (2018, May 9). *DMT | hallucinogen*. Encyclopedia Britannica. https://www.britannica.com/science/DMT

The Editors of Encyclopedia Britannica. (2020). Timothy Leary | biography, books, & facts | Britannica. In *Encyclopædia Britannica*. https://www.britannica.com/biography/Timothy-Leary

References

The Peterborough Examiner. (2020, May 12). *Thomas Chan told police he blamed stabbings on magic mushrooms.* Thepeteroroughexaminer.com. https://www.thepeterboroughexaminer.com/news/crime/2018/09/18/thomas-chan-told-police-he-blamed-stabbings-on-magic-mushrooms.html

Tibballs, G. (2006). *The world's greatest hoaxes.* (p. pp. 27-29). Barnes & Noble.

United States Drug Enforcement Administration. (2019a). *Drug scheduling.* Dea.gov. https://www.dea.gov/drug-scheduling

United States Drug Enforcement Administration. (2019b). *Mission statement.* Dea.gov. https://www.dea.gov/mission

Vecsey, C. (1991). *Handbook of American Indian religious freedom.* Crossroad.

Winstock, A. R. (2016, June 13). *Dosing for pleasure and why less is often more | Global Drug Survey.* Global Drug Survey. https://www.globaldrugsurvey.com/dosing-for-pleasure-and-why-less-is-often-more/

Images

Dondaldson, J. (2021). Shaman. In *Unsplash.* https://unsplash.com/photos/bhqsqkCowSk

FLY:D. (2021). Light trail. In *Unsplash.* https://unsplash.com/photos/3TtVnxJHfhw

Gatewood, H. (2021). Pills. In *Unsplash.* https://unsplash.com/photos/_jbClosDsD4

Johndrow, M. (2021). Skull face. In *Unsplash*. https://unsplash.com/photos/KAsjiTRuihk

Löw, V. (2021). Amazon forest. In *Unsplash*. https://unsplash.com/photos/A62nYytlz8M

National Cancer Institute. (2021). Laboratory. In *Unsplash*. https://unsplash.com/photos/VCLYhr-ZUEQ

www.ingramcontent.com/pod-product-compliance
Lightning Source LLC
Chambersburg PA
CBHW071816080526
44589CB00012B/814